THE LAYMAN IN THE CHURCH

and Other Essays

E. H. Schillebeeckx, O.P.

alba house

A DIVISION OF ST. PAUL PUBLICATIONS
STATEN ISLAND 14, NEW YORK

Nihil Obstat
JACOBUS J. CONWAY
Censor Deputatus

Imprimatur
+ THOMAS
Ep. Darensis et Leighlensis

31 August 1963

Printed in the Republic of Ireland

THE LAYMAN IN THE CHURCH

And Other Essays

CONTENTS

ACKNOWLEDGEMENTS

The publishers are grateful to the following for permission to reproduce material in this book:

Sheed & Ward Ltd and the Editor, *Life of the Spirit*, for "The Death of a Christian"

Sheed & Ward Ltd and the Editor, *Doctrine and Life*, for "The Layman in the Church"

The Editor, *Life of the Spirit*, for "The Second Vatican Council"

THE SECOND VATICAN COUNCIL

THE way in which the first phase of the second Vatican Council developed has surpassed the most optimistic expectations. It is undoubtedly true that constitutionally nothing has been decided, nor has a single conciliar document been definitively approved. *Denzinger* is as yet unable to adopt anything from this Council. And yet I feel that it has already passed the turning-point.

We know, as we always have, that the dogmatic significance of a college of bishops spread out over the whole world is the same as that of a world episcopate gathered together in synod. But experience here in Rome has shown that psychologically and sociologically these two manifest themselves in astoundingly different ways. Thoughts on the subject of the renewal and remodelling of the apostolate of the Church, which many a bishop in his see humbly kept to himself or expressed only with hesitation and caution, were at first only whispered diffidently in Rome, until people discovered that practically all their colleagues were thinking the same way. A moral harmony found expression which had been there all along without being put into words. The mutual contact of bishops, from so many lands and from all parts of the world, released what had obviously, and for a long time, been crying out for authoritative formulation. For that is precisely how we define a council.

Alas, some are bound to see these happenings exclusively in the light (or the darkness) of the opposition: conservatism *versus* progressiveness. They secularize what has taken place, though the 'worldly' element is undoubtedly deeply embedded here. Even while the Council was sitting there appeared a book of more than 600 pages, not obtainable through normal channels but distributed among the council fathers, with the title *Complotto contro la Chiesa* (Rome 1962), written by a certain 'Maurice Pinay'. In an extreme and absurd manner the book reflects what at the time of the Council was printed in some Italian newspapers: that the Council was a clever manoeuvre to push through the reluctant *apertura a sinistra* (the Italian idea of a break through). One passage is enough to illustrate this: '. . . a veritable fifth column of agents controlled by Freemasons, Communism and the secret powers that command them; some of these agents were even to be found among those cardinals, archbishops and bishops who form a kind of progressive wing within the Council and who are trying to get the various reforms adopted . . . and all this ostensibly in order to modernize the Church and to align her with the times, but with the hidden intention of opening doors to Communism, to hasten the collapse of the free world and to prepare for the imminent destruction of Christendom' (p. 1). But even disregarding this kind of reactionary nonsense, it is an over-simplification to characterize the council debates, which were conducted graciously and courteously, in terms of an antithesis between conservative and progressive fathers-in-council.

There is, however, no denying the presence of a spiritual demarcation within the college of the council fathers, but how to define the dividing line is another matter. Both sides labour with tireless devotion for the well-being of the Church, and as the line winds its arbitrary way through the world-episcopate it takes no heed of national loyalties, passing straight through most of the national episcopates whether they be Transalpine, Asiatic, or South American. Even Italy, Spain and North America are aware of the division somewhere in their midst.

On either side of the almost untraceable dividing-line people's thinking and working stems from the self-same faith, the Catholic and apostolic faith. And yet one sometimes gets the impression that the others are speaking from a faith apart. One is astonished to find oneself more in sympathy with the thinking of Christian, non-Catholic 'observers' than with the views of one's own brethren on the other side of the dividing-line. The accusation of connivance with the Reformation is therefore not without foundation. What is, in fact, happening then?

Two Worlds

For at least 63 per cent of the world episcopate (and I would call this a conservative estimate) the Church's salvation lies along paths quite different from those of the remaining 37 per cent, who in fact saw their way of thinking reflected in the prepared theological schedules or schemata of this Council. The experience of these bishops, who in their practical pastoral care are confronted spiritually and physically with the human and ecclesiastical problems of today, gave them quite a different view of the problems that were posed. It was heart-warming to hear for instance how Chilean, Brazilian and Indian bishops, involved in pastoral concerns and for that reason to some extent unaware of the development of trans-alpine theology, on hearing an exposition of some theological theme, would add the spontaneous comment, as if of one mind with the speaker, 'This really means something to us'. The living contact with human reality had given them that open-mindedness, which only needed to be 'filled', or sometimes just to be put into words. As against this there is not merely a theology, but a whole attitude of life and way of thinking among bishops and theologians who, for some reason or other (sometimes understandably), have lost or are likely to lose contact with the world or with reality. A 'world of ideas' stands like a screen between them and reality, and they are not aware of it. This world of ideas they see as the reality in which they live. This was the painful experience during the first phase of the Council. Certain bishops and theologians, whose concern is not pastoral and who, in some cases, have never had anything to do with pastoral work, are in danger of losing contact with the world.

This, I thought, was where the dividing-line could be found—where the one thinks essentially (and it is more than a 'way of thinking') and the other thinks existentially. This is, it is true, an over-simplification. But from the tenor of the original theological schemata and from discussions with these bishops and theologians it is clear that this is where the fundamental difference begins. The 'essentialist' attitude regards the mysteries of our faith and of human life as if they were abstract essences which, first and foremost, must be formulated as precisely as possible. Now I too hold no personal brief for vagueness and fanciful dreaming about the faith. The perspective in which the mystery is intimated to us must certainly be defined carefully if we want our faith to remain inwardly meaningful. But for the 'essentialists' something else is at stake. For them, apparently, the mystery is held in the grasp of their ideas. The exact formulation of an unchangeable *essence* was to be the main purpose of the Council. *Nella sua formulazione piu esatta*, that is how the *Osservatore Romana* summed up the Report or *Relatio* in which the scheme 'On the sources of revelation' at the nineteenth General Congregation was presented to the council fathers. It had become the main concern of the preparatory commission to formulate the faith as precisely as possible. As precisely as possible—this implied measuring, regardless of historicity, the content of the faith as an abstract esssence, like an immutable and measurable number (it used to be said of 'essence' that it is like a number). When essentialists speak of people, they do not speak of human beings but of 'human nature'. In speaking of the Church they mean a kind of precipitate, an abstract 'essence Church', which is one (and one cannot be two, or divided, so there is only one Church, which knows no division), and this abstract essence as such is placed in reality. The fact that this essence then finds itself in rather a strange world is so much the worse for that world, which will have to give way wherever this 'essence' makes its appearance. (The schema on 'Church and State' is very revealing in this matter.) That the world does in fact make way, but in an unexpected manner, for it turns away from this essence, they can only attribute to sinful nature. Is the Church not inevitably 'a sign of contradiction'?

Tragedy

There is an element of tragedy in this way of

thinking, in this attitude to life. On the whole, we tend to treat these people somewhat harshly, and in so doing we are drawing the dividing-line more sharply. It is not unwillingness on their part. They simply 'cannot existentially do otherwise'. For these people to think non-essentially means skirting the truth. Hence the consternation, even panic, when after the first large-scale vote it was found that the majority of the world episcopate had abandoned the essentialist mode of thought. So despite our heartfelt joy, any sense of triumph is unthinkable. And it is as if the council fathers were instinctively aware of this tragedy. For whereas in spite of insistent requests not to applaud, they repeatedly showed their approval of a speech by one bishop or another, of a speech that came straight from the heart or that went straight to the core of the problem, when the Pope—that magnificent figure—at the crucial point in the Council, recognizing the moral majority, ordered the theological schema on the subject of the sources of revelation to be removed, the papal announcement was heard in a moving silence. No applause, although the fathers could not contain their joy. One observer said to me afterwards: 'That silence was like the breath of God's Spirit. Applause would have spoilt the spiritual meaning of this Council'.

And yet there is something incomprehensible in this tragedy. How is it possible that these people, although existentially incapable of other than 'essentialist thinking', when confronted with the different mentality of the majority of the council fathers, do not even for a moment begin to doubt their own ideas? Surely the majority cannot all be heretics? I cannot understand this, and I do not want to understand it, for fear of being unjust. Perhaps this attitude is essentialist thinking taken to its ultimate and extreme conclusion, the conclusion that we are heretics.

Pastoral Care and Theology

So the first phase of the Council was a revelation, a bringing to light of something which was there, though originally veiled and latent. From the beginning the council fathers let it be known that they had not come to Rome to 'consolidate their positions' as some had wished, but to take a leap towards the future of the Church; *aggiornamento* became the watchword. Biblical, ecumenical, pastoral, these were the words that rebounded again and again from the walls of St. Peter's. I am not giving away any secrets when I repeat the newspaper report of how Cardinal Ottaviani gained his reputation for being a good loser. During the penultimate week of this first phase of the Council he presented his statement 'Concerning the Church' with the quip, 'Yes, I know what you are going to say: *Tolle*, *tolle*, take that statement away, it is neither biblical, nor ecumenical, nor pastoral; it is scholastic'. There was sympathetic applause. The cardinal went on to show that his statement was indeed pastoral, ecumenical and biblical. But for the essentialist these terms have a completely different connotation.

In any case it would be somewhat naive to attribute all disagreements to existential leanings on the one hand and essential on the other. The situation in the various sees of the world Church is so diverse that open minds will suddenly (or so it seems) turn reactionary or vice-versa when certain problems are raised. These pastoral bishops think pragmatically rather than theologically. Many of them are still subconsciously 'essentialists' (after all that is what they were brought up to be), but they have applied themselves heart and soul to certain practical problems, as for instance to the whole question of liturgical revival. It is possible to give these pastors practical guidance on matters of religious tolerance for example, without first stating a philosophic or dogmatic basis for tolerance. Life is more convincing than theory.

And then there are still some bishops each one of whom is a world unto himself—delightful museum-pieces, for whom time does not seem to exist. During the morning meetings in St. Peter's they murmur their rosaries, or have a nap, they say the offices during the opening Mass, or they visit the Blessed Sacrament at one of the side altars, and when they suddenly hear their name called, because their turn has come to address the meeting, they ferret about for their few sheets of paper and then, for precisely ten minutes, they say their piece, so completely out of this world that this is the signal for the Fathers' exodus to the canteen. Then the man returns to his seat, without any self-satisfaction, unconcerned, completely matter-of-fact, as if he had just been to close a window, and resumes his muttered prayers or dozes off to the sleep of the just. Saintly phantoms from long bygone days. But perhaps they are very near to the Lord, on whose gracious pardon this Council depends.

The Final Result?

Is it possible at this stage to surmise what the outcome of Vatican II is going to be? Yes, in principle it is. The majority have expressed themselves in favour of a different approach. This fact cannot be gainsaid. On the other hand, this majority is realistic enough not to want it all their own way. They will take the minority into account, and eventually some sort of compromise is bound to be at least the official outcome of the Council.

The Council is faced moreover with all kinds of unknown factors. In the first place there is the possibility that it might have to be wound up because of the death of the all-inspiring Pope John. On the other hand, no new Pope could ever pretend that Vatican II had never been—even if no officially approved document were available.*

Then there is the long interim period from 8th December, 1962 to 29th September, 1963. But the Pope has already seen to it that there could be no repetition of what has occurred in some preparatory commissions.

Finally there is in my opinion one other doubtful factor—the 600 bishops of the C.E.L.A.M., that is, those from the Latin-American and Mexican bishops' conference. They have been the top stakes, as it were, in the 'lobbies', to put it crudely, of theologians from both sides. They still have vulnerable areas which can cause them to veer one way or another. They are receptive to modern ideas and yet they are also a little afriad of them. In many respects they are also dependent on all kinds of authorities. In my opinion, we have here another unknown quantity, not so much in the

*This factor has of course been resolved by Pope Paul VI. Father Schillebeeckx was writing before the death of John XXIII.

young dynamic South American theologians, but in their bishops.

Completely unresolved still is the problem of the relationship between the 'collegiate' government of the Church (by the world episcopacy under the leadership of the Pope) and the 'central' government of the ecclesiastical Curia. I think that this problem is going to be the main issue of the second phase of this Council, if God grants John XXIII time to bring *his* Council to an end.

Our faith is still the old 'Catholic' faith, no other. But a faith that is alive.

MISUNDERSTANDINGS AT THE COUNCIL

We can only rejoice that after the turn taken by the second Vatican Council during its first phase we may justifiably hope for greater freedom for what is, somewhat erroneously, called the 'new theology' I have already commented on that aspect of the Council; we shall now consider some related aspects.

When we examine more closely the speeches of the council fathers in St. Peter's, we have to admit that some of the utterances of the so-called 'open wing' strike us as less felicitous, and such as might evoke, during the second phase of the Council, reactions of a kind that could easily cause confusion in the ranks of this 'open wing'.

The 'Open Wing's' Gain

We are all convinced that the 'open wing' carried

the day (and how mundane we are when we represent events in such terms, when in reality the whole of the world episcopacy is aware of the impulse of the Holy Spirit in God's Church). But I am convinced that the 'open wing' has won, not simply because it represented 'progress', but because it brought to the fore aspects of reality which had, apparently, remained unnoticed by the so-called 'closed wing'. It is always the germ of truth behind a certain trend, in profane matters too, that gives it its dynamic force and power of appeal. Untruth as such has no force of appeal whatsoever. But that is precisely why we must not forget that the 'germ of truth', upheld by the 'conservative wing', also possesses dynamic forces which might well, during the second phase of the Council, assert their appeal. And if in that case it is the truth, even only in germ, that elicits our response, we can only acclaim it. It is only the truth that sets us free. But there exists a very real danger that the bias of the 'closed wing' position would gain credence among many council fathers alongside the germ of truth it represents, just because this truth is vested in what I have called a one-sided 'essentialist' attitude. So it may be necessary for the 'open wing' to reconsider its own position if on 8 September 1963 'conservatism' is not to start off with a new force of appeal. Similarly the more entrenched elements should rethink their positions and move towards an inner 'catharsis' or purging.

The Term 'Ecumenical'

Undeniably there were misunderstandings during the

council debates, inside and outside St. Peter's, especially regarding the terms 'ecumenical' and 'pastoral'. In my opinion the word 'ecumenical' should describe an attitude of mind attuned in faith to a visible unity, not only of love and hope, but also of faith among all people who confess Christ as Lord, and in fact more generally among all people who acknowledge the value of the religious in human life. Because of their belief in the *Una Catholica*, however, the ecumenical attitude of Catholics has acquired a particular stamp. To them the term 'ecumenical' expresses the mind of Catholics who want to do full justice to the totality of their belief. This attitude has introduced a certain distinction between the uncontaminated essence of the Church, as Christ instituted it under the leadership of the apostolic office of the college of bishops headed by the Pope, and the empirical outward form of that same Church in which, through the ages of church history, all forms of one-sidedness could gain access, at least in its external manifestations. As a result certain Catholic values have become obscured in the Church's teaching, and more particularly in its practice. And it is precisely these obscured or neglected truths and values of the faith which (partly also by the inner logic of contrasts) are retained in their original authenticity in the practice of the non-Catholic Christian Churches, even indeed in some large non-Christian world religions, more fully than they are practised by the average Catholic. And that is why it is rightly the ecumenical concern of Catholics to emphasize those suppressed truths and values. In my opinion it was precisely this aspect of Catholic ecumenical thinking that, during the first phase of the Council, achieved an unmistakable break-through, more so than the 'new theology' as such. Not that one can really make this distinction, for the 'new theology' itself is motivated by an ecumenical spirit, and the re-integration of suppressed or overgrown truths into the totality of the theological synthesis is its hall-mark. A break-through for this ecumenical thinking is in fact a break-through for the so-called 'new theology'. We should realize, moreover, that the new theology is just as much concerned with the 'consolidation of positions' with regard to the deposit of the faith—but by a renewal which, since it seeks to reintegrate by means of a return to the sources, calls for a shift of emphasis. For the new theology holds that the Catholic Church, in order to hold its own today as a reality which appeals to people's minds and hearts, should overhaul its entire outward form and rejuvenate itself. This was indeed the basic intuition that made Pope John XXIII decide to hold a general synod.

The Roman Viewpoint

'Roman theology' on the other hand (I realize this is a simplification, but in view of the bishops' own terms of reference in their interventions in the Council we might as well keep the classification, for lack of a better one) seemed to put quite a different interpretation on the word 'ecumenical' during the Council. Somewhat to my surprise I heard this expressed most strikingly when a bishop in St. Peter's complained pathetically: 'But where is all this going to lead, if we are to suppress one Catholic truth in order not to offend our disunited Eastern brethren, and another so as not to upset the Anglicans, and finally if we have to preserve a mysterious silence about yet another truth to avoid further alienating the Protestants?' This intervention speaks volumes. Apparently, to Roman theology ecumenical thinking means 'eirenics': suppressing or at any rate soft-pedalling some Catholic truths, which might put the Orthodox, the Anglican, the Protestant off Catholicism.

Reaction of the Fathers

Unfortunately, some liberal council fathers have in fact encouraged this Roman interpretation of the majority view. But if that represented the ecumenical thinking of two-thirds of the council fathers, then the reaction from the side of Roman theology seems to my mind understandable, even justified. And then I should be glad that the Council produced such a reaction.[1] For no matter how much we ought, in the first place, to emphasize what binds and unites us in the one Lord, we must not gloss over the real differences with a false eirenism, which, after all, would be nothing but wool over the eyes of other Christians. I say the real differences, and in doing so I am making a distinction between Catholic and non-Catholic faith,

[1] I prefer to set aside here the more complicated question of whether it would for instance be morally justified from a Catholic-ecumenical viewpoint to declare an actually revealed truth as *dogma* at a moment that the inner life of the Church does not feel the slightest need for such a declaration, and which, seen from the other side, would consolidate the positions of separated Christian brethren *vis-à-vis* the Catholic Church.

and not between the latter and a particular Catholic *theology*.[2]

Nevertheless the fact cannot be gainsaid that some of the council fathers by their contributions have fortified Roman theology in its interpretation of the term 'ecumenical'. When in an interview with *The Gelderlander*,[3] Professor S. Tromp[4] was asked: 'Did you, all this time, think of our separated brethren?', he replied in no uncertain terms: 'Indeed we must try not to offend the separated brethren and we must try not to widen the gulf'. This faithfully represents the Roman position. Ecumenics here clearly implies 'not giving offence'. Consequently his following statement is entirely, and I believe rightly, in keeping: 'In my opinion we can best help to restore unity by stating simple and clear truths. In this way the distance will not be increased, but it will be seen more clearly' (*loc. cit.*). Quite apart from the subjective meaning which the affirmation 'simple and clear truths' in this context normally has, one nevertheless has to admit that the question of what is the truth remains central (within the bounds of charity of course). Some, for instance, would have liked the Council to keep quiet about the mysteries concerning our Lady so as not to offend other Christians. Quite apart from the question of how this could have been achieved without giving offence to

[2] For however much the faith itself is expressed in theology, the latter may still place an emphasis where faith itself does not, and in this way differences may arise, e.g., between Catholic theology and the Reformed confession (which is less sharply distinguished from 'theology' than ours is), whereas in both cases one and the same datum of faith is involved.

[3] Tuesday, 18 December 1962, p. 2.

[4] Father Tromp is secretary to Cardinal Ottaviani.

the East, such eirenism is bound to invite reaction.[5]

The Term 'Pastoral'

A similar misunderstanding arose in connection with the use of the term 'pastoral'. It is well-known how much the Pope of this Council stressed its pastoral character. The purpose is the re-affirmation of ancient truths in such a way that they appeal once more to the people of today. But here too is a danger of misunderstanding, and the council debates actually brought it out. Some seem to have interpreted the affirmation of the pastoral orientation of the Council in a purely *pragmatic* sense, a pastoral care which is less concerned with the truth, or at any rate the formulation of the truth, than with the fully existential experience of faith, for which a vague indication of the content of belief would suffice. I believe Professor Tromp is reacting

[5] Of course the 'open wing' was right to protest against a separate schema on the Virgin Mary, where this same council does not devote a separate scheme to Christ or to the Redemption. For although this schema on Mary may repeat *ad infinitum* that Christ is the one and only saviour and that Mary contributed and contributes nothing to salvation that is not Christ's gift and Christ's grace, the fact remains that the Council (the preparatory commission) has put the wrong emphasis and created the impression that a short (and on the whole well-balanced) synthesis of belief on the subject of the mysteries concerning the Virgin Mary seems more important than a statement of faith regarding the mystery of Christ (which was *not* provided by the preparatory commission). In my opinion a protest against a separate schema in this connection is more than justified, for such a schema (however well-balanced it has turned out to be) is bound to cause a shift of emphasis in the life of the Church after the Council. Surely the history of dogma ought to have taught us this lesson long ago!

against this point of view when he says: 'For me the primary pastoral duty is to give the truth' (*loc. cit.*). I would agree with this wholeheartedly. The question is, however, how one interprets this truth: essentially or existentially.

To give new, contemporary expression to a truth does not mean that we can first strip the truth of all human conceptions and associations, so that we can then, as it were, look it straight in the face and, after that, dress it up in its 'new look' attire. The expression of the truth is the insight itself into the truth. There is never a moment, not even a fraction of a second, in which we see the 'naked' truth. The new expression of the truth is not something accidental, but is involved in our very understanding of it. This presupposes, of course, that we do not regard the truth as an abstract essence, as though we could leave our human station in order to survey it from a distance. 'Roman theology' unmistakably leaves the impression that a certain scholastic way of formulating and expressing the truth is the only means whereby the truth remains true, whereas all other expressions of the truth would be 'pastoral' implying a diminished embodiment of the truth. This inevitably means that pastoral theology is identified with 'diluted theology' (a point of view which is encouraged by some second-rate publications). They do not seem to understand that expressing the truth in itself should reveal its pastoral character, that its pastoral character is not just a 'pious appendage' to an essentialist-abstract truth which as such is non-pastoral. For surely a Council is in its essence pastoral; a Council does not acquire this pastoral character merely as a result of a positive desire or a consideration of policy on the part of a certain Pope. John XXIII's desire has not given this Council its own pastoral context, which other Councils might not have had; he has pointed to a fundamental aspect of every Council, for the presentation of a saving truth is an intrinsically pastoral activity, the pastoral activity of the doctrinal authority itself.

So it is very healthy that there are elements from the other side in the Council, who are sounding a note of warning against a pragmatic conception of truth. But it ought not to remain the prerogative of the 'conservative' wing alone to sound this note. It is a real and fundamental aspect of a true pastoral objective to regard the truth as a saving force. But the truth must be considered in a non-essentialist sense. It seems not impossible to me that the 'conservative' wing, by a healthy insistence on the truth as a pastoral value, wants to inflict its essentialism as well on the council fathers. This would be fatal for the Church in our time, a Church that would continue to speak a language that would no longer be understood by anyone except those leading insular existences, quite unaware of what is going on in our world.

For there is a persistent belief that 'speaking in modern terms' entails speaking in old-fashioned language twenty-five years hence. So it does, since truth only emerges in a given historical situation. But to some people this assertion apparently conveys the illusion that there is, somewhere, a 'timeless language' which would never date; and this would simply boil down to the unspoken assertion that a definite moment in history (conditioned by history) and therefore a mere phase in history, a moment which by comparison with a previous moment was itself described as using modern language, is superimposed as a model beyond time and space for the entire subsequent evolution of the Church. Even if this were true (up to a point at any rate) to my mind it would in any case only apply to the phase which we call the primitive apostolic age, with its scripture, which still provides the universal exemplar. To refer back to a certain snapshot of Church history—even one taken at a peak period, as for instance the age of scholasticism—and posit it as a norm for all further insight into the truth is in fact a form of relativism 'maintaining the absolute truth', because it means that a relatively successful theological synthesis—and every human achievement is relative in this sense—leads to rejection of every new synthesis.

The fact that today's modern language is 'dated' tomorrow simply implies that expressing the truth is a never-ending task which has to be begun anew all the time, but it is quite out of the question that one could ever hope to promote a certain historical interpretation to the status of a timeless statement that could of itself provide an absolute formulation of the faith. This would mean pinning the truth through the heart instead of rescuing it, as we intended, from the tumultuous actuality of human life. This, it seems to me, is the painful mistake people make who think the Church 'must speak its own language' (which it must), but who then identify that language with one particular phase of the perennially new language of revelation. The Catholic Church must undoubtedly speak its own language, and it should not, in the name of eirenism, speak a language alien to it. But the Church's own language is the ever-changing language of the people, only cast in the idiom of the one revelation and also, as a negative norm, in the language of the Bible. It is surely significant that St. Thomas (who in his own time so boldly used 'modern language' in his theology) nevertheless says at a certain moment: 'We should not lightly abandon the language of the scriptures' (*de divinis non facile debet homo aliter loqui quam s.scriptura loquatur, Contra Errores Graecorum,* C.I.).

The Question of the Language

Up till now we have discussed the deeper sense ot the word 'language'. The question of language in its usual sense, of terminology in fact, is nevertheless closely linked with this. And in this sense Latin is quite often called the Church's own language. There are all kinds of historical reasons for this, and we ought not to underestimate its proven value. And I happily concede that the use of Latin has been a blessing durin*ʃ* the Council, not because the language was Latin, bu*ι* because Latin was the only language which was understood and to some extent spoken by all. The same could equally have been said of, for instance, either English or Italian, if either of these languages had been understood and spoken by all the council fathers. So it is not really a question of Latin as such, but of one language which is actually understood by all, so that there is less likelihood of misconstruing each other's words in dubious translations.

And yet it is typical that some see advantages not simply in Latin as a practical universal language, but Latin *an sich,* and more particularly as a 'dead language' which no longer develops spontaneously (except in *artefacta* or artificial neologisms). They are convinced that a 'dead language' is best suited to render the unchanging truth. Apart from the implications that the 'unchanging truth' is a 'dead thing', if it can so readily be formulated in 'dead terms', this assertion once again reveals a trace of an essentialistic interpretation of truth, which is as erroneous as the relativism in some modern trends. In our human thinking we must surely make a distinction between 'the truth as such' and the 'truth as known and believed by man', so that absolute values in our knowledge are safeguarded by the inner (if you like, objective) tendency of our relative, incomplete vision of reality which provides continuity between all our imperfect interpretations of the truth. It is precisely by focusing on the truth or reality from ever-changing positions that we safeguard an increasingly clear perspective of the truth, and that is why 'progressiveness' is a prerequisite if the fullness of truth is to be allowed the free scope that is its due. Conservatism, therefore, defined as adherence to one particular account of the truth (as if this were all-embracing), is by definition a violation of the truth itself.

We do not pretend that the newness offers safeguards because it is new. Neither the old nor the new as such can be safeguards of the truth. But a new point of view, a new sensitivity to its own environment—however much untruths may insinuate themselves, just as untruths also gain access to truths handed down of old—at least throws a new light on a truth and offers a new insight into a truth not previously discerned, or at any rate not formulated. And then it is quite possible that a 'dead language', which does not grow with the new sensitivity to the environment (for that is why it is dead), is *ipso facto* incapable of integrating the new aspects of reality—except quite artifically, and hence falsely, sometimes even dangerously so. A dead language is obviously suited to the formulation of those aspects which humanity had discovered at the time that this language was still a living instrument of their thought.[6] And it is just because of this that a dead language can quite naturally produce conservatism. Not that it enshrouds an untruth, but it enshrines a germ of truth in such a way that all further growth in understanding is seen as an accidental extrinsic addition, and thus by sealing off an element of truth which was discovered long ago (and still remains valid) it places it in a false twilight. Or take the expression: 'Essence is like *number*'. Every addition or subtraction makes it into a different number and so destroys the first 'essence'. Hence each new understanding of the truth leaves the old understanding essentially untouched, and is therefore merely a chance accretion, otherwise the first understanding would be destroyed. I often found during the council debates that the 'progressives' were only fighting against this sterilization of the truth, while the others thought that they were attacking the essential truth within. And so there was righteous indignation on both sides. This, to me, was more than sufficient—and painful—proof of how the bias of pure conceptualism (which goes hand in hand with essentialism)

[6] This, is of course, a consideration of only one aspect of the use of the Latin language. A wider consideration of this problem would bring many other aspects to light, placing the 'one-sidedness' of what I am saying here in a truer perspective. My objections apply mainly to the *exclusive* use of Latin in theology.

can hamper fruitful council debates between the 'open' and 'closed wings' and cause all manner of suspicion. Of course the 'open wing' is just as much concerned about the truth. It was extraordinary how one newspaper spoke of the 'orthodox or conservative group' as against the 'supporters of the open group' implying that the latter were not worried about the orthodoxy of the faith and unaware of the biblical assertion: 'The truth will set you free'.

Truth as Possession and Growing Truth

Cardinal Ottaviani, in an interview with a journalist of *La France catholique*, said quite rightly: 'Theology today is in a ferment, and there is a great deal that is by no means ready yet; nothing should be included in a dogmatic constitution that is not yet ripe'. I fully agree with this. But it is another matter whether a fossilized truth (which, I repeat, in so far as it is part truth, is true and remains true) still appears in a true light in our time, when it is presented with all its original circumscription. Here, I thought, lies a deep-rooted misunderstanding. Whatever earlier Councils, Trent and Vatican I, for instance, decided dogmatically rightly remains (now and in a hundred years' time) a norm for the Catholic faith. But a complementary truth passed over in silence perhaps at Trent, because of reaction or simply because this truth was not a matter of controversy, might well imply a more important and from a religious point of view more valuable aspect of truth than what Trent decided. Moreover the Tridentine aspect of truth might reveal its uniquely

Catholic significance only within the totality of this complementary religious truth. Surely then it is an inadequate procedure to go on repeating and re-affirming this Tridentine aspect, while concealing again the complementary truth? Consciously stating a part truth outside its totality always threatens to make it a heresy, an excision. It is quite possible to place a truth in an untrue light. To prevent this was often the sincere intention of the so-called 'open' wing, who were blamed for being in league with non-Catholic Christians, and for concealing truth from this motive. At this Council the Church finally broke with her counter-reformation attitude of mind, but not with her catholicity. And this is where the tragic misunderstanding arose in connection with the so-called 'two sources' of revelation. Admittedly the 'progressive wing' was at times compromised by what was written on all sides in inferior publications in the way of biased comments on various questions. But the pre-war crisis of Modernism should have taught us that all who used so-called modernist terms (for instance 'collective religious experience', said of the Church) did not necessarily interpret these in a modernist sense. And yet the judgment of Modernism was passed on unorthodox as well as orthodox. Authority should beware of repeating such painful mistakes.

The Basic Conflict

That Pope John XXIII should state that this Council must not re-affirm what has formerly been decided seems to have been an intuition on the part of a man who, especially through his priestly feeling for pastoral care, helped by his attitude of mind as a historian, was particularly sensitive to the complementary aspects of a historian, was particularly sensitive to the complementary aspects of a particular truth. Truth as a human 'possession' is never outside time and place. A denial of this (making one interpretation of truth absolute) betrays its fatal effect in what we have called essentialist thinking. This, I maintain, is the basic conflict that came to the surface during the first phase of the Council. The misunderstandings surrounding the ecumenical and pastoral attitudes of the Council are merely the outcome of it. And I trust that I am not exposing myself to the reproach of denying the value of human concepts.

If people would think all this over carefully, I would be in complete agreement with Professor Tromp when he says: 'I am hopeful that both sides will grow nearer together, that they will have a better understanding of each other and that they will find that their viewpoints are not as widely separated as they thought' (*loc. cit.*). Nevertheless I think that those beyond the Alps first need to understand what we mean when we attack the 'essentialist way of thinking', and that those on this side of the Alps should with a good grace learn to accept the sincere anxiety of 'Roman theology' to preserve the faith in its pure form. I fully recognize that the Church has need of a body which (at any rate by helping the Church's teaching authority, the college of bishops, headed by the Pope) is concerned with the *particular* care (I say particular, for every believer has this duty) of preserving the faith intact. But this purity does not only, not even primarily, demand the maintenance of what at one time has been dogmatically stated, but an increasingly shaded integration of what has been defined in the balanced totality of the faith. Without this it is impossible to keep the faith pure, because people will become obsessed with a part truth to the detriment of the whole.

If this remains the aim, the second phase of the Council will not be characterized by a schema *de fide pure custodienda* (for keeping the faith *pure* is the implicit if not explicit premise of all of us) but by the truthful schema *de fide vitaliter custodienda*—how can we in this age keep the true faith *alive?* Then the rugged back of the Alps will indeed have been broken.

THE LAYMAN IN THE CHURCH

THE purpose of this essay is modest: to sketch in broad lines the place of the *layman*, seen theologically, in the Church. A general view of the limits of what is possible and permissible, of what pertains to the laity and what does not, will guard us against breaking through dividing lines and will prevent our committing errors like the one frequently made, in connection with proposals for the coming general Council, that the diaconate should be re-established as an independent order and should be considered as the 'summit of the lay apostolate'. That the diaconate should be something more than a stepping-stone to the priesthood is quite justifiably desired by many people; but it is essentially a clerical state and can, under no aspect, be called lay-apostolate.

Translator's Note: Fr. Schillebeeckx's Dutch presents difficulties to the translator not wholly due to a foreigner's lack of familiarity with the language. The author's careful regard for theological precision, shown in the multiplication of qualifying terms (a syntax to which the English language does not lend itself), and the necessity, imposed by the originality of his thought, of developing his own vocabulary, combine to make the close rendering that is desirable in an article of this nature at times impossible. Where more or less literal translation has proved unsatisfactory I have tried to express what I judge to be the thought of Fr. Schillebeeckx, giving, where the importance or special intractability of the passage suggest it, the author's own phrase in brackets. Only the original article can serve as a basis for professional theological discussion; in it, too, will be found references to continental publications, the reproduction of which here does not seem useful.

THE CHRISTIAN IDEA OF LAYMAN

The Christian Term 'Layman'

By reason, not so much of the secularisation of society as of the laicist atmosphere in which this secularisation has been concretely pursued, the term 'lay person', as used by non-Christians, has usually for Catholic ears (in continental countries) an unfavourable connotation. In the period since the middle of the nineteenth century the sense of the term has swung from something like 'free-thinker' by way of 'anti-clerical' to 'non-cleric' and 'non-religious' (in the sense of one who is not a monk or a nun). In the nineteenth century the terms *société laique* and *enseignement laique* made their appearance, having the sense of not simply non-religious, but rather positively extra-religious, with the implication of anti-religious. In our own day, at least as far as the term itself is concerned, this unfavourable connotation has disappeared so that now even Christians can be quite ready to accept its use. Consequently, when we find in the new French Constitution: 'l'État est laique', this means, if we disregard subjective ulterior intentions that the state as such is concerned only with secular affairs and, moreover, is in this sphere autonomous. The confusion attached to the notion is such that, as late as 1945, the Italian Parliament witnessed the following exchange between a socialist and a Catholic deputy. To the demand of a socialist that a 'lay person' be appointed minister of education, the Catholic De Gasperi replied heatedly that there had never been any intention of appointing a cleric to this post. To which the socialist retorted with equal heat that his meaning was being twisted, that he was not concerned about clerics; by lay person he understood a non-Catholic.

The sense attached to the term lay person in theology derives very clearly from Scripture. When the Canon Law uses the term 'laicus', a lay person, in the sense of 'Christifidelis', i.e., one who believes, this has a remote basis in the Scriptures themselves. The word 'laikos' comes from 'laos', people. In profane Greek usage this signifies the people as distinct from the rulers and leaders of the people, thus as distinct from the ruling and intellectual classes. In the Bible this word has a more precise signification, being applied exclusively to the people of God as distinct from the Gentiles. The 'laos' is *the* people, God's people, that is, in relation to the Christian era, the Church of Christ. At the same time, nevertheless, the Scriptures use this term also in contrast to the leaders of this people of God, namely, in contrast to the priests, levites and prophets. The people or the 'laos' is that part of the Church that is subject to the leadership and control of the Church's hierarchy.

Going on to the word 'laikos', from which the words 'laicus', 'lay person', are derived: this signifies in profane Greek usage a member of the common class, belonging to the people but set apart from the leaders of the people. We do not find the word in this sense either in the Scripture or in the Septuagint, the Greek translation used by the Jews; but it is found in a few ancient Greek translations of the Old Testament. The sense in which it is used is important. *Laikos*, lay, signifies here the profane or unsanctified, that is, what is not consecrated to the worship of God. In contrast to the loaves of proposition, ordinary bread, which is not reserved for worship, is called simply 'lay bread'. Likewise, the area of the Temple is 'sacred', while outside the Temple is 'lay'. This distinction between 'sacred' and 'lay' again applies only to things *within* the people of God. But in early Christian writings this word is soon transferred to persons (see Clement of Rome), and so there appears the distinction between the terms 'klerikos' and 'laikos' or lay person within the community of the Church.

If we bring all these points together we gain the following result. A *lay person* is (1) a member of the people of God assembled in the Church, (2) but in this community of the Church he is set apart from the hierarchy, being attached to a distinct group, (3) on the side of the laity this separation implies a reference to the profane, to that, namely, which is not directly connected with the mystery of Church worship. With these data we are already in a position to say that Christian semantics, leading us to the significance of the term, 'lay person' *suggests* that the laity is characterised both by its *membership of the Church* and by its relation to *secular affairs.*

The Theological Notion of Lay Person and Lay Spirituality

The Church is the 'great Sign set up unto the nations that invites to her all who have not yet believed' (First Council of the Vatican; *Denz.* 1794). In another article (in *Tijdschrift voor geestelijk Leven*) we have pointed out that not only the hierarchy but all the faithful constitute an essential element in this great sacramental sign. The Church here on earth makes manifest on the plane of visible historical fact the grace of redemption; and this grace is nothing other than the person of Christ, dead, indeed, but now raised up to heavenly life. Of this mystery of grace the Church is the outward, human form in the shape of a social sign or, more exactly, in the shape of a community which is a sign ('societas-signum') (*tekengemeenschap*). Both in her hierarchy and in her community of lay believers the Church is the visible realization on earth of the redemptive grace of Christ. The hidden union with God in Christ granted by grace is revealed in, and brought about through, the external social sign of a community governed by the rulers of the Church. It follows that lay people in the Church form an essential part of the efficacious sign of grace (*werkzaam genadeteken*) and of Christ, ascended into heaven. This means that the visible and active presence of grace among us is brought about in two-fold fashion: in and through the apostolic office of the Church's hierarchy (institutional authoritative and charismatic fashion) and through the faithful who bear the characters of baptism and confirmation (fashion determined by the institutional role of lay people and by charisms).

In this complexus the hierarchy of the Church exercises a directive and authoritative function which exists, consequently, for the sake of the community of lay believers: this apostolic office is ministerial, a service of Christ and of the faithful. Nevertheless, the layman, placed though he is in a relation of obedience, based on faith, to the hierarchy of the Church, is, in his quality of Christian layman, truly and in full a part of the Church. He plays his part in supporting the visible and active historical form of redemptive grace in the world. This distinction between *clerics* (those belonging by the nature of their office to the hierarchy, namely, pope and bishops; or those participating in the hierarchy of orders, namely, simple priests or presbyters and deacons) and *lay people* in the Church is not to be explained merely as the result of historical or sociological development; it originates in the will of Christ himself and is not subject to change. This distinction is of the essence of the Church. It follows that one who actually, in one or other fashion, has an inner *participation* in the true apostolic office of the Church's hierarchy is by definition *not a layman:* he belongs to the clergy of the Church (concretely: pope, bishops, priests and deacons). It is true that the derived participations in this apostolic office (namely, priesthood and diaconate) were not directly instituted by Christ. Christ instituted directly the fullness of the priestly (i.e. episcopal) apostolic office. But the Church is conscious of her power to divide this hierarchical office in response to her needs into separate grades, as has been done, for example, for the priesthood and diaconate.

In the first place the layman in the Church is a *Christian*, a member of the Church, the people of God, the Kingdom of God on earth, for which he, too, bears a personal responsibility. Christ's command: 'Be ye perfect as also your heavenly Father is perfect' (*Matt.* 5:48), is directed to all men: pope, bishops, priests, religious and laity. To seek after the kingdom of God as after a hidden treasure or a pearl of great price, for the sake of which we must, if necessary, despise all things, is as much an obligation of the layman as it is of the priest and the religious—a life lived in communion of Christian life and of the Church. Charity, altruistically motivated and self-sacrificing, must necessarily therefore be the heart of a lay life too. In addition, the Christian life or membership of the community of the Church does not consist only in a personal relationship with God in Christ Jesus; it is at the same time, by the very fact, and *within* this dialogue with the living God, essentially apostolic. We are not meant just to *live in* the kingdom of God; we have imposed on us the task of extending the kingdom. This must not be misunderstood. As a lay member of the Church, as one, that is, who does not belong to the ecclesiastical hierarchy, the believer has a part in the *apostolate or mission of the Church*, but not in the mission or apostolate *of the hierarchy*. Looked at under the aspect of apostolate, the Church is a community with an apostolic mission, within which, however, is to be found a priestly or 'authoritative' form of apostolate side by side with a lay form of mission. Each of these is a particular form or manifestation of the single apostolate of the whole Church. The distinction between these two forms is a consequence of the distinction, established by Christ himself, between the clergy and the laity. This distinction between two forms of the apostolate is, therefore, itself of divine origin. Consequently, the line of demarcation between the two in the Church cannot be permitted to become indistinct. Recognition of the role played by the laity in the Church can never, therefore, acquire the sense that the layman is now to have a part in what formerly pertained exclusively to the clergy.

My only concern here is to clarify the basic principle of lay spirituality and of the lay apostolate in contrast to the apostolate of the hierarchy.

The ecclesiastical difference between the laity and the clergy can be based only upon the internal structure of the supernatural community, the Church. It is precisely because there is a *community* of the faithful, of laymen, a people of God, that leaders of this people are needed in the Church; a hierarchical authority. And since this community is a *communion in grace*, internally united by the supernatural bond of faith, hope and love, as also by the common bond of the same sacraments of the one faith, the authority in this community cannot be of natural origin: it must have authorization for its task from Christ, together with the charism that is bound up with such a Christ-given mission. As baptized persons, the laity as well as the clergy have therefore an ecclesiastical, sacred task. But the clergy fulfil this task as a principle of authority and leadership in a teaching, governing and sanctifying priestly activity, whereas the laity must have the same ecclesiastical sense of responsibility for the kingdom of God, but as God's people, without the function of authority and thus without the official priesthood. Thus the lay community too belongs to the historical, tangible stature in which the grace of redemption appears on earth: the earthly Church. By their incorporation into the Church, that is, by their baptism, the laity consequently receive a share in this real function of the Church: they receive, namely, the charge to give visible stature to the faithful communion with Christ in grace, in and through their whole life. Therefore every baptized person is conjointly responsible for the

Church and for its function as a sign in the midst of this world.

Now, it is true indeed that this ecclesiastical responsibility or mission, which the layman receives in virtue of his baptism, is given to a *man*, that is, to a person whose task in this world is to give meaning to his own life; to a person, consequently, who is also charged with bringing human order into the sphere of worldly life. On this account, through his baptism the faithful laymen receives at the same time the charge to *integrate* the earthly purpose of his life *into* his communion in grace with God in Christ. Thus the layman's earthly charge becomes part of his entirely God-centred attitude to life. One who is baptized, therefore, must integrate his involvement in the affairs of this world into his existence as a believer and member of the Church. In the very nature of the case, this means that the *typical* mark of the Christian lay status will be an apostolate carried on in and through direct concern with secular affairs.

In what does such an apostolate consist?

In order to determine precisely what the lay status is, at least in so far as it is a form of the visible embodiment of the Church in this world, we must always go back to baptism as the sacrament of our incorporation into the Church, and so, in Christ. Now, the Church is the historical and tangible form in which Christ's grace of victory visibly exists in this world. In and through the Church, the grace of God in Christ is present among us as an historical reality that we can grasp: 'a sign raised up among the nations'. Because of the Incarnation and its continuation in the Church as the earthly 'Body of the Lord', this tangible and visible form of existence belongs to the very essence of Christian grace. Grace, wherever it takes on a historical, visible stature, is 'the Church'.

If incorporation into this visible communion in grace is then the first and direct effect of baptism, the believer receives in and with his baptism the charge to take his part in the essential function of the Church: he receives the charge to give, in and through his earthly life, a visible stature to his communion in grace with God. The life, the entire life of the baptized layman must consequently become the *visibility of grace;* through every given situation and in every moment his earthly life must be a 'signum gratiae Christianae' (a sign of Christian grace). Only in this way can the responsibility be fulfilled which all who are baptized bear, together, for the Church and for its function as a sign in this world.

As a citizen, the layman is situated directly in a context of the worldly concerns (*in de 'diesseitige' dimensie*) of this earthly life, but at the same time, as one who has been baptized, namely, as a Christian layman in the Church, he has the charge to be 'the Church' *in* his worldly situation. In other words, however the Christian layman is placed in this world, the Church must find its visible manifestation in him: in his occupation, in his relations with his fellow-men and in his dealings with things, in his family and its integration in the society and the nation; in short, in the entirety of his secular life. This living, rooted in the world, as the concrete manifestation of his security in God's grace and of his solicitude for the kingdom of God, is *typical* of the Christian layman. We will analyse this further.

CHARACTERISTICS OF LAY STATUS

The world in which we live, the world of nature and history, goes back ultimately, not simply to the divine Creator, but more exactly to the divine Creator who desires to enter into personal relations with us. Through such personal communication with the living God our life in the world takes on deeper significance. Human freedom, to which God personally addresses himself, has also a creative function in respect of cultural values. Now, the fact is that God addresses us personally in order that we may find him now not merely indirectly, through natural realities and history, in other words, through our existence in the world, but that we may also enjoy direct, as it were vertical and immediate, relations with him in a personal intercourse with him, person speaking to person, even though it must be through the veil of faith without vision. God's personal design with us implies, therefore, that our meeting with God in his self-revelation as a person imposes as a basic requirement the raising of our eyes *from* the things of the world *to* God. It is precisely this elevation which must be given to the direction of our lives that naturally opens up at once the possibility, side by side with Christian life in the world, of life in the cloister. (This point will not be developed further here.) For the Christian layman in the world this means that even his orientation towards secular affairs can sometimes involve making sacrifices and that, moreover, the layman as a Christian must anticipate such an occasion and hold himself in readiness to make the sacrifice. His involvement in secular affairs can never have the last word. (Neither is further development of this point undertaken here.) But it is precisely this personal communion with God, who is at the same time the Creator, that requires that the secular occupation of the layman be carried out entirely within the context of this dialogue with the living God. Together with God, with whom the Christian layman has a personal relation in Christ and in the Church, the layman assumes his personal responsibility in the history of this world. In this way his dialogue with the world, his creative effort to make of the world a truly human dwelling-place, participates in his entirely God-centred attitude to life, participates in his dialogue with God. We Christians too easily show an inclination to leave to unbelievers the secular ordering of temporal society. We forget that concern for so-called 'profane' affairs, the recognition of mundane realities, is an authentic component of the entirely God-centred attitude to life. Secularization or laicizing in itself is a process that belongs within the Christian life, within the Church, a process within the life of the people of God. There is a certain ambiguity in these words. Their sense is this: that the believer, *within* his dialogue with God, is led to give loyal recognition to earthly reality too, with its own characteristically secular institutions. Christian 'secularization' is thus utterly different from atheistic laicization, which accepts earthly reality as the definitive and exclusive horizon of life. Exclusively profane or atheistic laicization is objectively a 'hairesis' (Gr: heresy); it is a tearing away of profane affairs, that is, earthly reality, out of the whole to which they belong for they find their true place only *within* the relation of existence and of faith which binds man to God. Only when it is placed outside this context is earthly reality 'profaned'.

This orientation towards secular affairs, what I may briefly call 'secular involvement' (*seculariteit;* Eng.: 'secularity'), is the foundation on which rests the specific character of lay spirituality and of the lay apostolate in the Church. It implies that the layman also sanctifies himself precisely in this secular involvement, and that his apostolic activity is carried on first and foremost through this secular involvement. A mother is a Christian as the mother of a family, a father as a father, a teacher as a teacher, and so on. By making his contribution to the work of the world, by co-operating, each in his own place, in the political, social and economic organization of temporal society, as tradesman, scientist or intellectual, the Christian layman places himself in a personal relationship with God. In this sense the grace given as a layman is 'lay' grace, just as it has female characteristics for women, and male for men: for it is from within his personal situation that each stands in personal relationship to God. A mother, for example, is placed in personal contact with God through her very motherhood too. This motherhood itself has a special significance for her existence as a Christian, just as her existence as a Christian has significance for her motherhood. With his whole human entity the layman enters personally into an encounter with God. Though the layman must raise his eyes from the world to God if he is to gaze full in his face, this does not mean that he must forget his earthly task as though this were an occupation from which God is excluded; on the contrary, it obliges him to realize consciously the religious dimensions of this earthly task itself. If he does this, his secular task too takes on a Christian and apostolic significance. It is *man*, after all, who is *redeemed* by Christ. And the entity of the man is not a naked soul; the entity of the man is that spiritual, personal being who, through his own corporeality and in communion with other men, exists in this world in order, in and through the humanization of the world, to humanize himself also. It is in all his concrete reality that this being is touched by grace and redeemed by Christ; not only in the kernel of his soul, therefore, but, beginning from this centre of the person, also in his relations to his fellowmen and, through them, in his relations to the whole world and to the history of the world.

But redemption, at the same time, lays a *charge* on us. In connection with the question which concerns us here, this means that the mundane task of the Christian acquires a more profound significance: it is co-redemptive. Through the ordering of temporal society men are made more receptive to grace and obstacles to salvation are removed. Further, the tasks of earthly culture become the incarnation of the Christian commitment, in ordering life in this world to bring it into harmony with the kingdom of God. Natural and cultural values must themselves be redeemed and by a redemption that is not deferred to the end of time but that enters into the context of their history. To achieve this is the particular charge, within his total existence as a Christian, of the layman in the world. I might call this: *apostolic secular involvement*, an apostolate carried on through responsibility for secular affairs as the characteristic charge of the Christian layman as layman. Conscious committal of life, proceeding from a spirit that is redeemed, to secular affairs within the dialogue with God; and so, in and through this secular task, opening the world to receive the Good Tidings; and, by speaking this Word, incarnating it in the world as a foretaste of the eschatological glorification of the body and of the 'new heaven and earth'. It is saints of this pattern that our world needs at the present moment —a new form of holiness must spread its light in the Christian layman's responsibility for this world—saints who grasp the dogma of creation in all its concrete significance. For *Church life* (*kerkelijkheid*) means more than what takes its origin from the ecclesiastical hierarchy. Church life (*kerkelijk leven*) is just as much whatever has its origin in the faithful, the people of God, as the fruit of their eucharistic community of grace with Christ. Secular occupations must share in this life of the Church. Culture and all that human existence in the world embraces is not merely culture, that is, a task for man as such. It is a task for man as he is constituted by God; namely, as a being who, even in his very dealings with this world, comes into contact with grace. The risen Christ has significance for our whole life, including its worldly implications. Just as the religious state of perfection within this world is a sign of the future of the kingdom of God, so the integral lay state in the world is a sign of how salvation exists *in* this world.

It will be seen that in this Christian conception of the lay state in the world the value of the work of human society is fully acknowledged. This conception liberates us, too, from the heresy of extrinsicism and individualism latent in the idea that one's disposition, a 'good intention', makes action good (*de krypto-ketterij van het extrinsecisime en individualisme van de gezindheid of* '*goede mening*'). The fact that an action proceeds from charity (*het caritasmotief*) is not, of itself, enough. Or, more exactly, business efficiency, expertise and scientific knowledge, a sense of responsibility for the organization of life in the world, all that the concrete task in temporal affairs essentially demands of us, must be absorbed into this God-centred 'good intention'. These are the earthly form and incarnation of the motive of Christian charity in the layman. Only in this fashion can the values of the material world be respected within the act of faith in divine creation. Only in this fashion, moreover, will the layman experience no break in continuity between his secular occupation and his Christian personality. It not infrequently happens that Christians think of their daily work, even though it takes up the principal part of their time, as something foreign to their being Christian; and so their state of mind fluctuates between an impression of the falseness of their lives as Christians, and then again of an incompatibility between their professional lives and their Christianity. The result often is that the layman either has only moderate interests in his religious practice, or else he swings to the other extreme and has less sense of responsibility and less professional zeal in work than the non-Christian, in the false belief, only half-consciously expressed, that his poor workmanship takes on Christian value by reason of his being in a state of grace and his so-called 'good intention'; not forgetting either that it accumulates merit for heaven. How utterly different genuine Christianity in fact is! One example will suffice: that of nursing or health care. For the Christian lay person who is professionally concerned in it, such health care, which forms part of the general providence of society, is not merely a particular function in the universal process of humanizing mankind in this world. Nevertheless, it is precisely in this context that this social service becomes a 'sacrament of grace', an instrument of Christian fraternal charity. It gives concrete expression to God's love for men in the temporal and tangible form of skilled medical service to mankind. It is an apostolate carried on through trained care of the sick. The giving of skilled medical care and assistance is itself an incarnate witness to Christ's personal love addressing itself personally to men by way of this care of the sick. Here the technical and scientific equipment of modern medicine with its care and services is placed at the disposal of apostolic charity: it *is* this charity in a visible modern expression.

It is obvious then that when we speak to God personally in prayer our task in the world is not something that must be passed over in silence. On the contrary, it should be a subject of conversation; not with the purpose of discovering in prayer more about the technical aspects of our secular work, for prayer obviously cannot teach us anything about that; but primarily in order, in our personal encounter with God, to realize in detail how this secular occupation fits in to the economy of salvation, in order to purify our intention and to arouse our desire of saving others. Whenever, in the course of the day, we are working together with God we may also speak to God about our work. The layman's life of prayer, which still must be truly *prayer*, acquires in this way a colouring different from that of, for example, the religious. His lay occupation is a form-giving principle of his lay spirituality. Even in his personal encounter with God the layman is not simply a Christian, with all the characteristic interests of a Christian as a member of the kingdom of God; he is also a *layman*. He stands before God in prayer with all his concern for this world. His desire is certainly to deepen his belief in the kingdom of God and to draw from prayer the strength to devote himself entirely to the service of this kingdom; still he must realize that his secular occupation is something which cannot be of indifference to the divine overlordship. It is precisely because the layman *personally shares*, through grace, in God's own creative love for the world, that he becomes conscious—and first of all in his prayer—that his secular occupation has a positive, divine, redemptive sense, a significance in the economy of salvation.

From this lay point of view, taking account, that is, of the laity's orientation towards secular affairs, the general Christian apostolic activities of the layman as *Christian* may also be clarified. Thus the function to be fulfilled *in the Church* by the Christian as one who is baptized, confirmed and strengthened by the eucharistic sacrifice, will also always be determined by the layman's characteristic position in the world. A suggestive example of this is the duty laid on the layman by the sacrament of marriage. In the family the preaching of the word of God, for example, is primarily the duty of the parents by reason of the function given them *in the Church* by their marriage, in so far as it is the marriage of people who are baptized. The layman must also be witness in his characteristically lay fashion, in word and action, to the Word of God. He may even be entrusted with the exposition of the

Word of God as a lecturer in theology, although the true 'kerygma' or 'ministry of the Word' (*Acts* 6:4) does not pertain to him, since it is part of the hierarchy's apostolate. Further, since the layman shares in responsibility for the salvation of the Church and of mankind, he too has *a right to speak*. There is place in the Church, as Pius XII indicated, for 'public opinion' and open discussion in which the layman may put forward his own point of view. In whatever concerns the salvation of mankind the layman too has a *right* to intervene both by word and by action. This right is based on the mission received from the Church by one who bears the characters of baptism and confirmation; it is based too on the charism of the Holy Spirit given him in connection with this mission from the Church. There can therefore be categories of people who become lay apostles and who devote themselves exclusively by vocation to all kinds of Church apostolate; but this will always be as lay people. Others, meanwhile, will employ only their free time to making themselves useful to the Church in some particular fashion, over and above their general lay apostolate. The hierarchy, as guardian of all that pertains to the life of the Church, has consequently the obligation to respect and encourage the characteristically lay form of Church life. A layman, especially if he is an intellectual or has received some form of higher education, has his own view about several aspects of the Church. Exerting *moral* influence, he can from time to time assert himself vigorously. The very fact that he is a layman opens his eyes to aspects which perhaps escape the notice of the hierarchy. Whenever he complains about the cultural inertia of Catholics the

Church ought to listen and weigh his comments on their merits. But in all this specifically lay Christian activity in the Church the laity never act in an *authoritative* capacity; that is the prerogative of the hierarchy. This implies that the entire lay activity of a Christian in the Church falls under the control of ecclesiastical authority. This means likewise that the entire activity of the layman in Church and world can in no respect really participate in the hierarchical functions of teaching, government or pastoral care.

Is not this last statement explicitly contradicted by the various forms of Catholic Action which has been defined as 'participation by the laity in the apostolate of the hierarchy'?

This requires close attention. After a first and still tentative period in which, during the pontificate of Pius XI, the phrase 'lay *participation* in the hierarchical apostolate' was in fact employed, this terminology later disappeared completely from papal documents on Catholic Action and the lay apostolate. In these there is now mention only of 'cooperatio', *co-operation*, of the laity with the hierarchy. This is not simply a question of words. For lay co-operation or collaboration with the hierarchy alters in no way the lay status of the layman and consequently (the term) points at the same time to the characteristically lay sphere in which such co-operation is to be exercised. It indicates too the limits of this co-operation, making it clear that the layman can co-operate only as a *layman*, and therefore by reason of his specifically lay apostolate; and that, consequently, he can never 'play' the lay-pastor or the lay-deacon. *Apostolic secular involvement*, considered precisely as organized co-operation with the clerical apostolate, remains therefore the specifically lay contribution in this collaboration of the laity and the ecclesiastical hierarchy. The priesthood and the diaconate alone are genuine *participations* in the apostolic office of the ecclesiastical hierarchy; but precisely by reason of this participation priests and deacons are no longer laymen; they are clerics, even if they wear secular clothes and even in the event of their being married. (This point of view does not date only from the pontificate of Pius XII; we can find it already explicitly proposed by, for example, Clement of Alexandria and Origen who make a clear distinction between the laity on the one hand and the episcopate, priesthood and diaconate on the other.)

Immediate *co-operation* of laymen, on the contrary, with the ecclesiastical hierarchy, even when it takes the form of a full-time occupation and consequently requires that a person give up his secular place in the *world*, remains, in the category of the occupation of the *layman* in the *Church*. (This is contrary to Karl Rahner's opinion on the matter, but is in conformity with Pius XII's address to the last Lay Congress in Rome.) This category corresponds ultimately to what in the early Church was the sphere of the minor orders and the sub-diaconate (at that time a minor order). These orders are of their nature *lay*, but their functions constitute direct co-operation with the apostolate of the hierarchy (although at the present time these orders, at least in the Code of Canon Law which is always subject to change, are considered simply as steps to the diaconate and priesthood and consequently, *on this account*, are also called clerical). Such lay functions, carrying with them an obligation to co-operate with the hierarchy, therefore, by their very nature do not require ordination, but simply an ecclesiastical nomination, or mandate, from the hierarchy. (Up to the early Middle Ages the minor orders and even the sub-diaconate *were never conferred by an ordination;* an ecclesiastical nomination sufficed. In later times, by analogy with the diaconate and the priesthood, this nomination or mandate was accompanied by an ordination which, consequently, is not a true sacrament but simply a sacramental.)

The desire, expressed by lay people and priests, that laymen who devote their whole lives to such an organized form of apostolate in Catholic Action should also receive an *ordination* is theologically unjustified. It is obvious that laymen who, for example, on the missions *in fact* fulfil the functions which pertain to the apostolate of the diaconate should be made eligible for the order itself and so by ordination should become clerics. But ordination is never just a formality! What we now call Catholic Action is, therefore, nothing other than a *modern* form of the old idea of the "minor orders"; namely, the function in which a lay believer gains competency and mandate to collaborate directly with the activity of the hierarchy. This co-operation can, in accordance with the needs of the Church, take on many shapes; in the course of the Church's history its forms have undergone various changes. The following are some examples: assistance in public worship, acting as sacristan or altar-server, the administration of Church property, keeping Church accounts (this was not infrequently entrusted to subdeacons even in the Middle Ages), acting secretary to a bishop or priest, as a member of the choir, as a reader at church services when there is no deacon. Besides these, all sorts of new and modern forms can be suggested: lay representation among the officials of the diocesan court, lay agencies which would be commissioned by the ecclesiastical authorities to undertake religio-sociographical studies directed towards achieving better results from the hierarchical apostolate; assistance in governing the Church in so far as this government requires various specializations: canonical, theological, philosophical, sociological and so forth; (so, for example, a great deal of the work now done exclusively by priests in the Roman Congregations and in all sorts of Church activities and organizations, could be handled by laymen); further, organizations of laymen for the formation and instruction of Christians in view of their own lay apostolate in the world, namely, in the family, in the professions and trades, in the public life of the State, and so on; or again, lay organizations to uphold the rights of the Church in public life, or laymen who act as full-time leaders even of organizations with a specifically religious purpose, etc. etc. I might be able to formulate it as follows: it is a question, not of lay *participation*, but of lay assistance, in the exercise of the apostolic function of the ecclesiastical hierarchy. In other words, the rendering of *lay assistance*, whether to the teaching authority of the Church, or to the governmental functions of the Church, or to the sanctifying and pastoral duties of the priesthood. Lay assistance: this signifies consequently co-operation with the apostolate of the hierarchy *in so far* as the latter necessarily includes *secular involvement*. And this secular involvement penetrates deeply into the apostolate of the hierarchy which must of course direct itself towards contemporary mankind with all its human problems, which become problems too for the apostolate of the hierarchy of the Church.

This whole set of problems can no longer be surveyed without the co-operation of the laity who, with their competence in secular affairs, can throw a great deal of light on these matters. It was to just such lay people, devoting themselves full-time to this kind of apostolic activity that the minor orders were given in the early Church; that is, these people were appointed by the Church in this way by their official function. Since it is a question of co-operation with the specifically hierarchical apostolate, clearly the hierarchy, although making an appeal for professional work pertaining properly to the layman's competence, always maintains immediate directive control over this form of the lay apostolate (in contrast to the general lay apostolate). For in such co-operation as this with the hierarchy lay apostles place themselves in complete dependence on the ecclesiastical hierarchy to the immediate service of which they dedicate their secular skills. We can put it this way: the common general lay apostolate moves in the sphere of the world, but as proceeding from the apostolic spirit of a Christian and a member of the Church; it also moves in the sphere of the Church, but there as proceeding from the lay position of one who is baptized and confirmed. Lay co-operation with the apostolate of the hierarchy, on the contrary, moves in the sphere of the ecclesiastical hierarchy, *at least in so far* as this sphere includes secular involvement, that secular involvement which is the proper sphere of the layman.

So we see that the Christian layman bears responsibility both towards the Church and towards the world, and that his apostolic secular involvement is at the service of both Church and world.

Possible Dangers of the Present-day Awareness of the Christian Laity

We must accept fully the consequences of this lay spirituality. This growth of awareness demands a certain realignment of mentality also on the part of clerics. *Insight* into the specific role of the layman is not sufficient. It is *said* easily enough that the layman must assume more responsibility, but from the moment that laymen actually do this and put forward an opinion quite different from one held by the clergy the alarm bell is sounded in parish and religious houses. In the light of lay experience certain new emphases will sometimes be laid, perhaps even certain aspects in the faith will be brought to light which formerly were not wholly apparent to the clergy with their specifically clerical experience. Besides all this, from the moment that two Christian adults come into contact with one another in the performance of any task, even if one has a position of authority while the other truly possesses a spirit of obedience based on faith and submission to the Church, then it is in the course of nature that friction can no longer be avoided, just as friction between pastors and their bishops cannot be wholly eliminated. It is naturally true that, by reason of the still brief history of Christian self-awareness of the layman in the Church, the laity do not yet know exactly where the limits of their active function in the

Church lie. I should say: they do not know this because the theologians themselves do not yet properly know it, and because this whole new experience has not yet been fully thought out on the theological level. In these circumstances it need not surprise us if the layman, conscious that he holds his own place and significance in the Church, will sometimes here and there act as though he were the vicar and successor, perhaps not of Peter, but at least of Paul, the unruly one.

We must give the laity time and room so that they may feel their way, guided by the Church and enlightened by the theologians (not necessarily priests), towards their own function in the Church, moved as they are by the charism of the Holy Spirit. Now and again mistakes will be made in one direction or another. The clergy themselves, in their attempts to define their precise clerical task, have at times been guilty of thoroughgoing 'clericalization' and so have moved outside their own territory. They must not, then, be waiting to pounce if, in his turn, the layman now and again 'laicises', or even tries to 'clericalize' himself and act as though he were parish priest. Nevertheless, these are the two principal dangers which the layman must be on his guard against. On the one hand, that in his loyal recognition of secular reality, in whatever sphere it may be, he will allow himself to become so absorbed in secular involvement that he will forget the dialogue with God, and, through his sympathy for the institutions of the secular order, he will lose his feeling for the breath of the Spirit who sometimes breathes out over all institutions. And on the other hand, the danger (which threatens primarily the second form of lay apostolate) that the layman's collaboration with the hierarchy will lead him to arrogate to himself clerical airs, that he will take up an attitude as though the day of the priest in the Church were now ended and as though he, the layman, were now the one to assume care for the salvation of men and of the Church; the danger, in a word, that the layman will consider himself emancipated from the hierarchy.

All the same, that does not mean that the layman is simply an executive of official Church decisions. The layman has his own choice which is itself *of the Church;* he has his own task to fulfil which is of the Church. This is a consequence of the mandate of a baptized, confirmed and married Christian. This mandate, that through the eucharistic celebration of the whole Church, and hence of the layman himself, is continually stimulated and nourished in charismatic fashion until it is activated in word and action which are the expression of his hidden union in grace with Christ and with the whole Church. It is precisely for this reason that in Canon Law too the special activity of the layman in the Church should be given canonical *protection* just as, for example, the special pastoral activity of a parish priest is protected in the Code against possible abuse of episcopal authority. Until the dogmatic notion of the Christian laity is also given canonical structure the layman remains powerless, and, after enduring as many conflicts as he can support, throws over the whole enterprise. Such canonical protection does not involve any partial withdrawal of the laity from ecclesiastical authority. On the contrary, it is canonical, authoritative recognition of the particularly lay form of membership of the Church which belongs to the Christian layman. This canonical legislation might well be one of the proposals for the coming General Council.

Much more should properly be said about the full dimensions of the *Christian-being* of the layman, and about the full range of the *lay-being* of the Christian. Further, we should like to contrast the position of the layman in the world with that of lay people who are in religious orders (not priests) and with that of laymen in secular institutes. But this article was intended simply as a general survey. I should like to conclude by stressing once again the fact that the lay believer also belongs to the 'great Sign that has been raised up among the nations', a Sign confronted with which men must experience that there is something afoot in this society which calls itself the Church of Christ, something that so intrigues them that this society becomes for them a truly irresistible invitation to enter into it themselves or to live in it more fervently and more consistently.

THE DEATH OF A CHRISTIAN

THE OBJECTIVE FACT

Throughout the course of the growing development of the kingdom of God, the death of a Christian has taken a well-defined and important place. The ending of the earthly life of a Christian man is an essential phase in the coming of the kingdom of God. What I propose to do in this essay is to analyse the meaning of this phase placed in the whole of Christian eschatology or expectation of the future. I shall first examine death as an objective occurrence in Christian saving history, and then subsequently show how we Christians should personally experience the event of death in an eschatological attitude of mind: in other words what the answer of our life to death will be.

In the Dominican rite of interment, we sing 'Let us be glad and rejoice on this wonderful day God has made, on which he has called one of our loved ones to himself'. The day of a man's death, which has already seen a flood of despair in many a human heart, the Church, in her serene eschatological optimism, calls a joyful birthday on which we see the true light of life.

But if in a Christian view of death we are to avoid the untrue and the counterfeit, then we must take into account all the real aspects that make death a complicated issue. For this reason we must first examine death from the natural point of view, according to what we can know of it by natural knowledge alone.

Death Approached Through Purely Natural Knowledge

In itself, death is a normal and natural biological event: a necessary result either of the bodily organism wearing out, or of disease or external violence. The event is a sure indication of the limitedness of man in the earthly world. The graph of life follows a curve, coming into and disappearing from this tangible world. Death proves that man, at least corporeally, is a piece of nature, bound up in the transitoriness of the material world. Seen in this light, death is the clearest manifestation of the limitedness of the human condition. Such was the approach to death in the time of the patriarchs of the Old Testament: death was then considered a completely natural, normal and unavoidable fact in human life, the reasonably peaceful termination of a well-filled, meritorious life which must however know its coming and its going. This is the spirit behind, 'Remember man that dust thou art and unto dusty thou shalt return'. The Genesis story of Abraham's death is serenely simple: 'Abraham breathed his last in a good old age, an old man and full of years, and he was gathered to his people' (*Gen.* 25:8). There is in this no question at all of any reflection on the absurdity of death (revelation however is only in its initial stage). The same calmness of expression is found in the passing of other patriarchs: 'He breathed his last'; 'He drew up his feet on the bed and died' (Isaac—*Gen.* 35:29; Jacob—49:32). To die is simply a fact of human limitation, or, as it says in the book of Joshua, it is 'to go the way of all the earth' (23:14). In this primitive stage of reflection on death the ideal was, as

Judges says, 'to die in a good old age' (8:32). Such seems indeed to have been the first primitive wisdom of mankind concerning death. There is no explicit thought of a life continued hereafter.

When however the Jews were overcome with misery, and earthly political life became more problematical and more dramatic, they began to delve more deeply into the profound meaning of the great events of life: the agony of a mother giving birth, the problems of hard toil and sweat for sustenance, of suffering and of death. Holding to a religion which enjoyed the special leadership of the living God, the reflection of the Jewish people began to discover in death a history of the misery of the Fall that in its extent and profundity far exceeded any notion to be found in the idea of death as a mere result of the limitation of the human condition. However, within the religious reflection of Israel, there was also an implicit philosophical consideration of the facts, without which religious reflection would not have been able to bridge the gap between a purely natural notion of death and death seen immediately as a punishment for sin. We must now extract this implicit philosophizing from the religious context.

I have said that naturally speaking death is a normal, bodily, biological event: a bodily full-stop that as such does not tamper with the personal value of the soul of man or concern it directly. To be born, to grow and gradually or even suddenly to disintegrate are for a biological organism natural occurrences that pose no grave problems. Nevertheless, if we consider the death of a *man* and keep in mind the intimate oneness of man and come to the conclusion that the activity of a human person is intimately bound up with incarnation in its own bodiliness in this world, then the phenomenon of death becomes a fact that is difficult to digest, unintelligible and even absurd. Death (naturally speaking) cuts off a human personality from all its possibilities, because all the activity of a soul is directed through, and situated in the material world by means of its bodily incarnation. By the fact of the body's falling away, the soul becomes as it were inescapably confined (in contradiction of the Platonic doctrine) within its own bounds; it loses its situation, so that on purely philosophical grounds we must hold that death means a thorough cessation of activity for the whole man, a condition of spiritual lethargy and isolation. Still speaking naturally, we come to the conclusion that with death human life collapses in a complete fiasco—a senseless, absurd outcome. Because of a pointless biological occurrence, for example the opening of an artery, or a road or railway accident, the human person itself enters an existence of dreary emptiness. Something is not right; there is no proportion between the biological occurrence and the resulting solitary confinement of spiritual, personal reality which vastly surpasses the biological in worth and is in itself independent of the biological. Because of this absurdity there has arisen through the ages a whole literature of protest against death, which is either presented as a constructional error in the work of creation, or else as the end of everything—which again is contradicted by all sorts of irrepressibly strong suggestions pointing towards a person's continued existence after death by the continued life of the soul. The salutary promise that lies within the soul as something spiritual, something which rises above all that is merely bodily and throws vistas of eternity before itself, is drowned in tears shed over the unavoidability of dying and in the frightened awareness that the soul must inevitably slip into oblivion. Certainly quite a number of biological factors are also at work in the uneasy fear of death: think for example of the situation in a bombardment—of the biological fear from which even animals in their instinctive efforts to preserve life do not escape. With man however, and certainly in his reflections on death, the causes of his experiencing the reaction, 'It must not happen', lie much deeper than on the biological level. They are tied up with the depths of his existence as a spiritual person who along with other persons extends his personality in the world and to the world in love and justice. If we face this fact of the death of a *man* in all its rigour, and leaving aside any context of supernatural faith try to study it in purely philosophical terms, we really do land ourselves with a very thorny problem. On the natural level the death of man is indeed an absurd phenomenon, senseless and unintelligible, something that denies all the promise that man bears within himself in his earthly life and shatters all his innermost hopes. Apparently pure philosophy cannot say more about man's death. But such a philosophical judgment is crippling.

This points to the manner in which the history of the Fall and of salvation has an intimate effect on philosophy itself, and indicates too that a philosophy outside a Christian religious context must, when all is said and done, waver between two conclusions, one pointing to the significance of the existence of God, and the other, because of the absurdity of death, seeming but to make this conclusion once more problematical. For some the uncertainty will be cut through in the direction of a philosophy of absurdity which grows into 'atheistic existentialism'. Others who do not reason away the significant indications that God exists, but who appreciate them in synthesis with the objective date of the religious experience of the whole of mankind, will look upwards from the question mark that is written at the very centre of philosophy—will look up to religion: will the problem not perhaps find its solution there? Now we as Christians know that it is precisely revelation that casts a new light on the phenomenon of death, for, as the Fathers of the Church have already noted, revelation not only makes God known to man, but also makes man known to himself.

This brings us to the second point.

Death as a Datum in the Religious History of Fallen Man

In the second phase of revelation, the post-patriarchal period from the times of Moses to the sapiential books, there is already to be found a first explanation of the phenomenon of death. The book of Wisdom says: 'For God made not death: neither has he pleasure in the destruction of the living' (1:13; see also 2:24 *Ezek.* 18:23, etc.). It is moreover typical that some clarification of the notion of immortality should come in the Old Testament in the same books as those in which man came to the knowledge that a religious tragedy lay at the origin of death.

Revelation here teaches that God would fulfil the promise of immortality that lies confined in the human soul in the state of grace, if man would remain 'walking with God in the Garden', as Genesis puts it; that is, if man would truly allow God to be the living God in his life. It was in some way by religious reflection on the absurdity of death that the Jews, who believed in the intelligibility of all the works of Yahweh, came to compose the Genesis story of the fall into sin. God perfected his revelation *in* this reflection. St. Paul summarizes this divine revelation in the striking words: 'By one man sin entered into the world, and by sin death' (*Rom.* 5:12), and the Council of Trent determined that the punishment aspect of death is a dogmatic truth (*Denz.* 788, 789). The absurdity of death lies in the fact that man by his own sinful fault landed himself in the situation of the Fall: in other words, man himself, by sinning, made his own situation of promise into an absurdity. The absurdity does not come from God, it is not a constructional error in creation, which as God made it was good and perfectly intelligible. Sin itself is absurd, and death is punishment for sin. Not indeed a subsequent punishment, as for example an earthly court might impose a sentence of death. Sin itself kills. Sin affects us to the very root of what we are; it is the letting go of the living God and therefore the germ of the collapse of man. It is 'sin to death', as St. John says. Death is thus the empirical, visible appearance of sin: it is the revelation, in unmistakable visible clarity, in a painful historical fact, of the living God in a sinful man; for although death is an intrinsic consequence of sin, precisely as such it is also a sanction of the just God: in other words, the rebound of God's majesty and holiness in a sinful man. Death is the visible sign of the blameworthy situation of fallen man: 'You are children of death'. And so we understand that the punishment of death includes not only the decay of the body, but also the immediate consequence of this, the empty, lonely, shut-in-upon-self existence of the separated soul. Sin in itself is an absurdity freely willed by man, which spawns its own proper consequences. The death of an innocent child, fratricide, the death of a beloved mother whose love and care is woven into the texture of the whole of life, any death at all, proves only that there is something unstuck somewhere in the world, that something is maimed—something that cannot be explained by pointing philosophically to the limitations of humanity. A *man's* death means more than just a biological event, more than just the breakdown of a heart that cannot hold out any longer. It is the own manufacture of sinful humanity. A man who in his possibly sincere pride cannot acknowledge the fact of his own sinfulness, a man who abolishes the awareness of sin from human experience cannot see any sense in death and will logically pay homage to atheism. 'God made not death', Old Testament revelation says with serene simplicity. Death is a sentence of doom that man because of his sinfulness called down upon himself and all mankind. Death is sin itself in its corporeal visible form: it is the cutting off of self from God and all his creatures in a sickly existence of reversion to self, a metaphysical confinement; 'an eternal death', says scripture and the liturgy. The condition of a separated soul, entered upon by dying, is a just interpretation of what the religious moral phenomenon of sin is and of what it means finally to cut one's self off by denying God: sin is an act in which a man contorts himself aainst the objective order, inverts every thing, twists, perverts, betrays and forces all to bow to himself as to the pole of ultimate desire. The empty existence of the dead is as it were the wearied-of-life, forced inactivity of a man strung up by his own hand on the gibbet of sin, a besotted sleep without the hope of fresh dawn. *Mors aeterna*, in other words, a genuine hell. Thus sin is the manifestation in a sinful man of God's majesty and holiness and at the same time a *mysterium iniquitatis* of diabolical and human sinfulness'.[1]

This does not yet however bring out the definitive meaning of death. Revelation goes further and shows us how the living God himself perfected a saving mystery in that guilty and absurd experience of man.

Death as a Phase in the History of Christian Salvation: Christ's Death

Death is and remains, for the Christian too, a punishment for sin. In this sense death is and remains, for the Christian too, a terrifying machination of the devil who did not only tempt one man to his death, but all humanity, and even God himself, when he dared to become man. Nonetheless when this happened death itself entered into the kingdom of God. The last absurd

[1] In order not to complicate the question more than can be helped, we omit here the nevertheless important biblical revelation according to which death is a partner in covenant with the devil: death is an expression of the devil's sphere of power over earthly things (cf. *Gen.* 3; *Wis.* 2:24; *Jn.* 8:44; *Heb.* 2:14).

scandal of the tyranny of death, the death of the man Jesus who is God, in fact brought life back to humanity, because whatever the living God touches becomes itself alive, even though it be very death.

There are people who damage or destroy everything they touch, but there are others who manage to leave everything with which they come into contact, whether it be with their hands or with their reason, with their mind or their heart, somehow changed for the better. That which seems banal and everyday becomes with them resplendent with a new fascination which most would never have dreamed it possessed. So it is an incomparably outstanding way with the man Jesus, the God-man.

God himself, in the man Christ, has come into a humanity become absurd on account of our sins, into our humanity existing as it does in the fatal condition of the Fall. The living God, who as man has a right to unconditional immortality of the body, willed to become man in the concrete sense of the word. 'The Word was made flesh'. 'Flesh' here does not merely imply he became true man, but man in this fallen condition.

St. Paul says God took upon himself the 'body of sin' (*Rom.* 6:6): although sinless himself God came as man into a human existence which is marked with the sign of sin—death. St. Paul dares even to say 'He was made sin for us' (2 *Cor.* 5:21), not as if he himself had sinned, but rather because he died our death of punishment for sin. God has undergone death itself as the foremost embodiment of sin. In stark reality the man Jesus experienced corporeal death in all its horror, the powerless emptiness of the body's end.

Christ himself bears witness to the fact that the death he died is a death for sin. For this he came into the world. It is also clear from the fact that his death was the result of the sinful intrigues of the Jews; his death was an unmitigated murder, man laying violent hands on the Son of Man. It is clear too from the words of Christy's dying prayer: 'Lord, why have you forsaken me?' He experiences death in its mysterious darkness. In his warning to the weeping women, Christ grasps at the heart of death: 'Weep not for me, but for yourselves' —that is, weep not so much because of death' but rather for the soul that lives in death; weep because of sin. His death was death to sin (*Rom.* 6:10).

Death is something that we men by our sins have ourselves invented. Death is truly something man-made. And this man-made thing we have given to God. We can give God many things, but all that we give him is his already. Death alone, product of man's sin, was the only thing that God did not possess. We were certainly not to be envied in our unique possession of it. Yet in the effrontery of his sinfulness man knew the bitterness of presenting death to God on the cross. God's love for us must be overpowering—that the living God should have wanted to become truly one of us men just so as to be able to accept that painful gift. For one has to be man and God and at the same time love man overwhelmingly, outrageously, to be able to accept, and lovingly to long to accept, such a wretched gift at the hands of men. But it is precisely in this that a miracle occurs, far more wonderful than the miracle of Cana. If the devil has known of it, says St. Paul, he would never have allowed the Son of Man to be crucified (1 *Cor.* 2:8); however, he adds, this divinely wise plan of salvation was more than the devil's powers of understanding could hope to grasp.

But how does the death of Christ give death a new meaning? We have stated the reason already: by the fact that Life, the living God, came into contact with death. Such a contact was however no automatic occurrence, like the bringing together of a positive and a negative electrode so that a spark jumps to life. Christ insisted on the fact that he was giving his life freely to the Father, out of redemptive love for man (*Jn.* 10:8). His death is a sacrafice, an active self-dispossession and self-detachment for love of God—a death therefore diametrically opposed to the self-seeking of sin. Such a sacrificing love is the radical opposite of sin. The reality we are getting at here is a religious act of the man Jesus, his total experience of God expressing itself in the giving up of his life out of a perfect appreciation of God's superiority. We are redeemed by Christ's death as a loving sacrifice, not by Christ's death as a welter of pain and suffering.

The agony of Christ's death is not of God's doing, for here too the word of scripture is true: 'For God made not death: neither has he pleasure in the destruction of the living' (*Wis.* 1:13). The drama of the cross is not so much a scourge from above as the breaking through of God's merciful love into a torn and sinful world of men. It is the sinful world that makes the break-through of divine mercy in the man Jesus have the character of suffering and death. The redemption is thus the point of contact in this world between divine love descending and the fatally unsound condition of fallen man. Christ accepted death freely and for love, so that his death became the visible expression, the moment of realization, of his perfected love which in death was made indeed truly sacrificial love. That which before was the outward visibility of inward sinfulness, death, now in Christ becomes the visible manifestation of the highest possible awareness of God, the proof of God's superiority in the deed that was a total forsaking of self. Christ's death is the loving attachment of himself to God in visible abandonment, the free acceptance by a man of the terrifying abandonment of death: it is giving self over into the hands of God in the full awareness that in the supreme crisis of human life salvation can be expected only from him. 'Father, into thy hands I commend my spirit'. That which was the embodiment of the inward state of sin becomes in Christ the living expression of inward holiness, state of grace, and redeeming love. Thus the abandonment and the absurdity of death is intrinsically turned into an event which, though in itself crippling and as it were annihilating, nevertheless becomes the passage to an encounter with the living God: the Father in mercy receives the soul commended him. That which by itself led to the 'solitary confinement' of the soul by loss of the possibility of all natural contact with persons and things, becomes now a new life in the embrace of the life of God. The soul, cut off from the proper context of its life, lives now in a new context: it lives the very life of God. *Vita mutatur, non tollitur*. This is a pure gift of God, which will receive its full perfection in the resurrection of the body. It is the gift of divine life that penetrates right through to the bodily life of man'.[2]

[2] The resurrection must be considered in intimate unity with the Christian meaning of death, so that even death as a sacrifice of love is seen not to be the ultimate answer to the problem. The ultimate answer comes from God alone: it is resurrection.

Death is therefore in Christ no longer a *mors aeterna*, but a provisional though decisive phase of redemption, a passage to resurrection, an ascension to true life, a birthday. 'Death, I will be your death', are the words the liturgy places on the lips of Christ on Good Friday. By his death he destroyed death.

So by the fact that Christ, as a holy man who is God, entered lovingly into it, death has obtained a redemptive worth. Death remains a punishment for and a consequence of sin as a result of which Christ died; but the punishment now becomes reparation, satisfaction and meritorious penance. The punishment is now a constructive, salutary punishment; it receives something that of its own self it could not possess and has got only through God's merciful intervention—a positive saving worth.

We can now appreciate that as nothing escapes his providence, in the mind of God from the very beginning death was caught up into the highest plan of salvation. The absurdity of death never did exist in its own right, but only as drawn into the victory of Christ who overcame it. This is a picture of death in its objective reality. It does not yet tell how or whether *our* death, my death, can come to mean salvation. The glorious significance of our death is to be considered below.

OUR PERSONAL APPROACH

Dying is not an Act, but the Attitude of Mind in which we accept death can give it the value of an Act

The salutary worth of Christ's death, as we have

said, does not lie in the mere biological disintegration of a man who was at the same time God, but rather in the obedient love through which Christ sacrificed himself in absolute attachment to God. Death objectively and factually implies the abandoning of all; a thorough rooting out and dispossessing of self, a passive being-shut-off from without, a loss of proprietary right to self. Death takes everything from us. This precisely is the nature of death as a punishment for sin.

Death is something that happens to us; in itself dying is not an action done by man, let alone the greatest action he does: it is something which overcomes us. Death can therefore only have a positive, Christian and salutary significance when we freely accept this alienation from self, which is a fact, as a positively desired detachment from self for the love of God in union with the dying Christ. In other words, the attitude of mind in which we die gives death the power to take on the value of an act. We must, that is to say, possess the same spirit of sacrifice that inspired Christ when he made the sacrifice of his life (see *Phil.* 2:5-11). Only he who loves God above all things, with all his soul and with all his strength, is permitted to enter into heavenly life. Every little remainder of self-love must have disappeared from our heart. Our death can be the great action of love in which the most radical self-detachment is perfected through free acceptance for love of God. Death to a Christian is not therefore something done to him, in which he is merely passive, as if death's salutary worth were a kind of happy chance that falls upon him. On the contrary, the Christ-like acceptance of death is the most important action any Christian has to perform in this life.

First, dying must be a deed of obedient love, an act of adoration. *Fiat voluntas tua*, humble acceptance of God's intervention in our life, as and when he wills. Next, death must be an act of perfect contrition: death must develop into the religious experience of a sinner who feels the near approach of the holy God who can be seen only by the 'pure of heart'. Just as Christ in his agony saw in spirit unfolding before him the sins of man, and trembled, much more at the contrast between all that evil and the all-holiness of God than at the death which it was to produce, so also must the dying Christian bemoan with a contrite (crushed to pieces) heart not only his personal past sins, but also all sin and all evil in the world, and 'crying with a loud voice' call for mercy, as did Christ. *Dignum et iustum est:* that which is happening is just and fitting, for I, however holy I may be, see myself in solidarity with all human-kind. Third,[3] the adoration of God and loving contrition must grow into a genuine, salutary penance, into the experience of death as the uttermost self-denial for love of God, in union with the death of the Saviour: being emptied of self in union with Christ. Death is our most lonely moment: a dying man is cut off, uprooted, the great solitary who knows time and earth, loved ones and friends, fame, prestige and success, all things and everybody to be slipping away, and who comes at last before the one thing necessary, the One who judges all. 'My God and my all': this is the frame of mind in which a Christian ought to die.

[3] In these three points no more is intended than to give a brief schematic analysis of what takes place as a single unity in the actual event of death, in the manner of a religious experience, rich in grace and salvation, for a sinner who believes in Christ.

This acceptance of death can be so complete and intense in a Christian that it expels every last vestige of self-love, so that through death his soul without passing through purgatory comes immediately face to face with God. The Greek Fathers teach us that 'to see God' in the beatific vision is conditional upon ascesis and perfect purification from self-love, so that at the moment of the disappearance of the last trace of self-love, the beatific vision wells up spontaneously as if from within, in our very being purified by grace, as if the bursting open of the bubble of self-love made visible the deepest reality of our true 'I', God himself. In this light we can begin to understand the longing of some saints: *Cupio dissolvi et esse cum Christo—I long* to be released (from this life) and to be with Christ. Death in this spirit becomes a journey to an encounter with Christ: serene acceptance, even though in the midst of bodily torment, of this disclosure of self through which we give our life into God's hands, and hope for salvation from him alone. The Christian experiences the gratuity of redemption most strongly in death: *non ex operibus, sed ex gratia.*

We can now appreciate that to die a truly Christ-like death does not lie within the power of mere humanity: that the cry of sacrificing love uttered in death is not the stammering of our own voice, but the voice of the Spirit of Christ, who, as St. Paul says, whispers in us with inexpressible sighs 'Abba, Father', which we in our sacrifice try to emulate. To die is an act of grace: that is, by the power of grace a Christian turns the disintegration of his body into an act of religious sacrifice in union with Christ's redeeming purpose. 'No one has greater love than he who lays down his life'.

Daily Practice in Acquiring the Attitude of Mind in which we Must Die

The spirit in which we ought to die should normally be a condition resulting from our life as a whole, and must therefore be acquired by practice throughout life. This is not merely a kind of scarecrow thought raised up because of the possibility that we might die suddenly. Sudden death is certainly a real possibility, and therefore scripture warns us to be the watch: *Estote parati.* Still, the spirit of self-detachment which culminates in the free act of love, accepting death, is the constant and fundamental condition for Christian life and not only for the moment of death.

In the first place it remains ever true that, even in the case of Christians, death, biologically considered, is an 'accident', something absurd that can happen to us at any moment of our life. Death comes 'as a thief in the night' (cf. 1 *Thess.* 5:2), says St. Paul. As a biological reality death remains something that happens to us blindly. In Christian faith we know that death is not a blind accident, or rather we know that this senseless accident is providentially caught up into God's plan of salvation: God calls the soul to himself. In that instant the eternal lot of man is decided. His life's choice is fixed firm for ever. Some rather platonically-inclined theologians deal with the question as though death were not only a biological cessation but also, naturally considered, a spiritual act in which a man as it were recapitulates his whole life and fixes his fundamental choice for ever. Death itself would then be a human act, having in it an essential element of spiritual activity with the element of biological decline: a sort of spiritual undoing of the complete self by means of and in the collapse of the body. It is extremely difficult to reconcile this platonic view with sound psychology. It is of faith that with death the earthly pilgrimage (*status viae*) is definitely over, so that no further merit is possible since man has reached his final condition (see *Denz*. 457, 464, 493a, 503-531, 693). Nevertheless, the end of the state of pilgrimage does not come about by means of a spiritual act by which a man would sum up his life, and in an all-inclusive final decision spontaneously fix his choice one way or the other for ever. If we keep to the objective facts, we must say that the fundamental choice which at the time actually determines a man, is made rigidly firm at the moment of death; it is fixed for eternity precisely because of the falling away of his body. Because man can be active and constructive about his own personality only through the body, death naturally speaking puts a stop to everything. The existing life-orientation of a man is snapped off and bound rigid by the biological accident that robs the soul of its 'situated being', and so takes from it all its scope for activity.[4] This means,

[4] The fact that a soul which after death is revivified supernaturally in the beatific vision nevertheless remains fixed in its choice in spite of the revival of supernatural activity (in God) that it then enjoys, is due to the fact that the soul rests perfectly content in its final object, God, to whom it holds fast in happy and indissoluble possession. For a soul which after death does not immediately possess the vision of God (a soul in purgatory) there is also no possibility of a fundamental new choice, but then within the fixed basic orientation there is still possible a purifying process of spiritual growth: such is the particular significance of the doctrine of purgatory (which we do not now need to examine further).

in the Christian providential view, that a man's attitude of life is stabilized eternally as a result of the intervention of God, who in his wisdom and goodness decides upon the moment of death. This precisely is the profound meaning of the scripture which says: 'death comes as a thief in the night'. God does not ask us about our attitude of mind at the instant of death merely, but rather about our faithfulness to him throughout our life. The past is irreformable: it is impossible that there should be an instant in which we can escape from time and re-establish our past under a new light—not even the instant in which we die. As long as we live, the only light we have is that of our faith and of our existence in the world and in time. There can be no question of an act of recapitulation. Whatever during his life a man has made of the whole of his life, that he is at the moment of his death. It is true indeed that a man, precisely because he is free, can at any moment in his life give it a new fundamental orientation, however difficult it may be to do so. The fundamental choice which a man makes in the perspective of good or evil is not an act made once and for all. Because of his freedom and his ambiguous situation a man can at any time sacrifice his basic religious decision: the fundamental decision of will is on earth never a definitive achievement. It becomes such only by the loss of corporeality: in other words, by death itself as a disintegration. And providentially this means that God himself puts the term to human choice. God intervenes unexpectedly, and the life's choice at which a man has arrived at the moment is by his intervention fixed immovably for ever, as it were from without. Needless to say, in the presence of death

Absolute Good makes a more pressing call on the freedom of man than was usually the case during his life. All the more because to die in a state of grace is a special gift of God. God will speak to the personal freedom of a man in the last conscious acts of his life with greater urgency, to enable him if need be to give his life a new orientation. But this is not at all the same thing as a kind of recapitualtion of life in the moment of death; it is a possibility that man bears within himself at every moment of his conscious earthly life, but of which he very probably becomes more aware in the hour of death when the relativity of earthly values strikes him more forcefully. The attitude finally achieved is decisive, but this itself depends to a large extent on earlier attitudes which prepare the way for the final one. The significance of this in connection with our salvation lies in the fact that we must live in the realization that at any moment our orientation of life could be eternally decisive. For not we ourselves, but the living God, decide upon the moment in which the concrete attitude in which we are living is to pass over into eternity.

The fundamental orientation in which we establish ourselves throughout our life and which in the awareness of approaching death will very likely become intensified, corrected or even perhaps radically altered, is that very one in which, through our biological break-off, we are fixed for all eternity; it decides us for heaven or for hell. The basic attitude of mind of a man who in spite of weakness and betrayals of trust is nevertheless fundamentally orientated towards God, will, when death overtakes him in this condition, bring him to heaven. Whether or not our death is to be

Christ-like and salutary is therefore a question facing us throughout life. Our entire life is given us by God to test our love, as an opportunity to bear witness to our love of God and man and to allow our soul to mature by means of the sacrifice of self-detachment. The essential and inevitable detachment is death. For precisely this reason Christian ascetism, suffering and sickness, the misery in human life, are all aimed at inviting us to self-detachment, in order that our death might eventually have a positive and Christian meaning and be accepted spontaneously in disinterested, self-forgetful love of God.

In the light of the Christian meaning of death, the sacrifices and the miseries of life become a preparation for a good end. Death, suffering and misery remain always the product of sin, in themselves undesirable, the work of the devil, a curse. And still with a tender and fatherly hand God holds this work of destruction in check, and redemptively turns the very work of evil into a bitter yet salutary and necessary medicine. The fact is simply this, that later on we will not be able to see God face to face, if we do not truly love him with all our heart and with all our mind and with all our strength. Such an act of love implies a radical self-forsaking. Experience, however, teaches that an ordinary man, even with grace, does not normally by himself have the strength to carry out this demand for radical self-detachment. For this reason the divine finesse comes to the aid of our weakness through suffering and death. For though God himself did not invent suffering and death, and although it is to be reckoned to the account of sin's sentence of doom, still God from the very beginning has caught up suffering and death in his providence. He converts the very consequences of evil itself into the certain means of salvation, so that we, who would not have the courage to take the initiative in the necessary purifying of our lives can get the purification we need by free acceptance of what in any case it is not possible to avoid. Suffering and death itself become thus the supreme loving attention of God who desires the salvation of all men. For this reason many who 'know not the Christ' come eventually to the God of Christians through their anonymously Christian acceptance of suffering and death.

Continuously to work at liberating ourselves from self-love in order to do good is to work at making ours a truly Christ-like death. In this spirit it is then more or less an incidental matter whether we die suddenly, or after a long unconsciousness, or in such disheartening pain that any act of prayer is for the moment made impossible. Death itself is, when all is said and done, not an act. So if the soul on account of pain or unconsciousness in the biological break-down is no longer able to act, the inward, consolidated basic attitude of life remains a fact really present, the soul itself in its acquired personal religious worth, though for the moment it cannot express that worth in any action.

The personality which God then judges is the one that has been built up with the help of grace to a religious worth in all the previous activity of life. *Estote parati.* It is, of course, not true that God in his justice spies upon man to strike him down and make him die at the moment when he has just perhaps committed a mortal sin, nor is it right to think that God in his mercy seeks for the death of a sinner just that moment in which he feels a bit homesick for heaven and begins to be sorry for his evil past. We dare make no judgment about God's predestining love. Every man he calls as he wills and at the moment he freely determines. We do know, however, that God sees the whole man, the person, and therefore especially his basic attitude which can lie deeply hidden under 'sinfulness", for a man in his free power of action can sometimes be hindered by a mass of quite unforeseeable factors, but even so he can inwardly desire the good. For many after all sin rather out of weakness than out of wickedness. This does not however prevent the degree of Christlikeness of our death and therefore of our heavenly holiness from being normally speaking largely in proportion to the degree to which our life itself has been Christian, even though the merciful grace of God can sometimes bring about astonishing conversions in the conscious hour of death.

The thought of death must therefore be an enlightening idea in our lives. Above all, in this spirit, death—not ours but that of our loved ones—will be one of the most salutary detachments we shall experience in preparation for our own death: it makes us realize that here a man passes through the most bitter suffering he can bear, but that at the same time his belonging to God's grace can be experienced most vividly. Very often one sees that the death of a loved member of a Christian family means a powerful surge of divine grace in the family. Though they be crushed—for death remains death, something that should not have been, every loving heart will agree—in spite of the blow they experience more intimately than ever that they are in the hands of God. For the dying Christian this awareness can be so intense that death itself truly becomes for him a peaceful going to sleep in the Lord: like the unnoticed fall of a ripened fruit, he lets himself go and falls into the arms of God.

In life's process of detachment from self the very thought of death can be a stimulating factor. Death is like a light that is cast upon the whole of life, throwing the essentials into clear relief against the shadows of all that is of little importance. One can pretend and act a part all one's life long, but it will very seldom happen that there will be any pretence in death: then all pretence is stilled, all mimicry dumb, and with the approach of the end one comes all too often to the knowledge that much of life was but a worthless lie. This is precisely the reason why there must be a vital retention of the thought of death during life. Every moment of our existence must be lived in the spirit that will enable us to sacrifice our life for love of God. 'I die daily', says Saint Paul (1 *Cor.* 15:31), for 'I bear the death-agony of Christ in my members'.

Christian Death as the Beginning of the Eschatological Resurrection

The Christian's thought of death is anything but a sombre nightmare. Certainly the sacrifice as such always means self's irretrievable loss of self in the courageous generosity of love. In this, only the crippling disintegration falls certainly within experience. The reward of the sacrifice lies on the far side of its pain, so that faith's certainty of finding self again in God rests purely on a divine gift, and is not to be found accounted for in the biological suffering of death, which as such is experienced as a purposeless destruction. Christian death however gives us a joyful Easter promise, thanks to Christ. God's acceptance of the sacrifice of love, the Resurrection, is an intrinsic factor in death, not only for Christ, but for us too. Thanks to Christ again, our death in sacrifice is in principle our resurrection too. The Christian idea of death as a sacrifice is therefore no damper on life, but an enlightenment that places everything, even the smallest detail, in its true perspective. 'Death is precious', not only to the dying but to the living too.

In a death accepted in the Christian manner, we see clearly that to die is but the first phase in an eschatological, future-facing event: it is the loss of self, but only in order that we may receive ourselves more gloriously than before, a pure gift from the hands of God. Death is only the passage to eternal life, the beginning of resurrection. For each one in particular death is already the end of the world, and so is the individual's first step to the return of Christ, for this return means nothing other than the universal resurrection of the body through which the saints will enjoy the perfectly human encounter with the risen, visible, victorious Christ, and those who are damned will also be excluded in a bodily manner from the glorious kingdom of God. That which death deprived us of by disembodiment, our corporeal earthly entity and our immediate inter-human relations, is given back in overwhelming abundance as God's gift in the resurrection: in the 'new heaven and earth' and in the intimacy of reinstated human relations in the communion of saints.

In this eschatological perspective we can appreciate that death is an event concerning not only the individual, but taking place in and concerning the whole kingdom of God. The liturgy for the dead therefore makes the whole company of heaven come down to meet the departed: 'May God's angels lead you to paradise, may God's martyrs meet your coming. May they all receive you into their midst, into the heavenly city'. The eschatological triumphant character of Christian death shows us that the glory of Thabor is a possibility present in every moment of our earthly life.

Christ's glorious transfiguration on Thabor was in a certain sense possible only because during his earthly life he already bore death within his heart and spirit as the loving sacrifice of his life. Whoever lives in this way—with death in his heart: not death the gloomy curse which kills, but death blessed by the sacrifice of the living God—is able to live constantly in the spirit of Thabor, in which there is even place for light-heartedness and joy. For after the last supper just before his death Jesus said to us: 'These things I have spoken to you, that my joy may be in you, and your joy may be filled' (*Jn.* 15:11). 'To die is gain' (*Phil.* 1:21).

The Sacraments as Incorporation in Christ's Resurrection from the Dead

Before we conclude, something must be said about the sacraments. The blessing of Christian death lies in the linking of our death with the death of Christ, so that his life becomes our life in the blessed vision of God, and in eventual resurrection. The linking of our death with Christ's death takes place precisely in the power of the faith we show externally in the sacraments. We take care for the Christ-likeness of our death by anticipation in the sacraments experienced in faith. Saint Paul says, 'There is no condemnation to them that are in Christ Jesus' (*Rom.* 8:1). The sacraments already in principle overcome death in so far as it is a curse. For the sacraments incorporate us, not in a dead Christ, but in the risen Christ. In the *memento* for the dead we pray in the Mass: 'Be mindful, Lord, of thy servants and handmaids who have gone before us in the sign of faith and who sleep the sleep of peace'. The sign of faith, *signum fidei*, is the patristic term for baptism. Our baptism immerses us in the death of Christ and is therefore a guarantee of Christian death and thus of resurrection, at least for those who live according to the promises of their baptism. And that which is begun in baptism, which is nourished and strengthened in the Eucharist as the sacrificial partaking in the dying and risen Christ, and in particular ways deepened and stressed in all the other sacraments, will at last find its visible and real completion in our bodily death. By the grace of our sacramental life of faith, our death is made Christian. Whatever in Christian death is painful and ugly, full of dread and destruction, is reckoned to the account of our solidarity with sinful humanity: it is the work of man. But the richness and the hope, the living power and the light that shines out of death is the pure work of grace, the consequence of our sacramental encounter with Christ. The sacraments, especially the last anointing and viaticum, are the mediaries through which the living God smiles upon the dying across the last grim sneer of sin, which would like if it could to triumph in this death but instead is literally crushed out in it. 'Death is swallowed up in victory' (1 *Cor.* 15:54).

It would be possible to illustrate all the facets of death, as we have examined them above, from the whole of the liturgy for the dying and the dead: the prayers for the dying, the Mass of the dead, the funeral service and the burial. The objective stature and the personal experience of death are moreover clearly illustrated in the three crosses on Golgotha. Two men are hanging, one on the left, one on the right of the crucified Christ. Two men rebelling against death and its hopelessness. But one of them struggles around towards the dying Christ . . . and what he sees and realizes is enough to give him complete understanding of his own death.

Some Practical Considerations about the Christian Attitude Towards Death and the Ceremonies of Burial

It should first be pointed out that, because of the Christian importance of death, every man has the right to know when, according to human reckoning, the final moment is approaching, to give him the chance the better to prepare himself. That his doctor or his family should keep the fact from him is pointless. Rightly enough, the information has to be given most tactfully and delicately and after reasonable preparation, but simply to hide the true state of affairs betrays a very sorry appreciation of the power of faith. For the same reason it is unChristian to delay the last anointing to the last possible moment or leave it until the sick man is unconscious, in order not to frighten him. Not the last moment, but the first real indication that sickness might be fatal is the time to administer the last anointing: the sufferer has nothing to lose by it—on the contrary.

It may be helpful to say something about the things done around a death-bed and at a funeral. The most important thing is that in these things our faith in the Christian salutary value of death is made obvious. I am not thinking so much of the class distinctions that the world still expresses by the manner in which it deals with the man who in death had appeared naked before his God. This is a problem that can be solved only by considerateness, patience and above all by education. The real point at issue is that whatever the ceremony, an interment must be a witness to Christian faith concerning death. How often does it not happen that the terms in which notification of death or letters of sympathy are couched are merely natural or even heathen? However strongly bitter sorrow is felt—and it always will be felt—the atmosphere surrounding death must still be an expression of the prayerful hope that the living, loving God will take the soul to himself. *Credo in vitam aeternam.* No symbols of despair, no broken pillars, no scythes, no hour-glasses or skulls and crossbones. Are these the symbols of a Christ-like death which is but coming to life in Christ the Saviour? A funeral should be a serenely solemn farewell to a loved one who departs into life. Generous, genuine Christian manners are demanded, not a masquerade. The important thing is the spirit in which the ceremonies and the style of the funeral must be fashioned or accepted. True enough, one cannot brush aside all at once the tyrannous protocol of death imposed by the undertakers. This calls for gradual alteration. But it will be possible only if Christians are more intimately aware of the meaning of death and at the same time feel within themselves more effectually the apostolic urge to call out in the face of the world, and most certainly in the presence of death, life's greatest problem, that we Christians have a clear solution for this problem through our faith in Christ the Redeemer, our faith in the kingdom to come, our faith in Life—the eternal life of God.